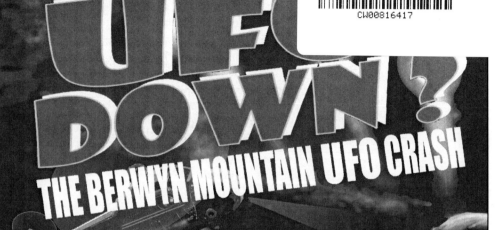

UFO DOWN?

THE BERWYN MOUNTAIN UFO CRASH

ANDY ROBERTS

Edited by Jon Downes
Typeset by Jonathan Downes and Liv McCarthy
Cover by Roger Hutchinson
Layout by SPiderKaT for CFZ Communications
Using Microsoft Word 2003, Microsoft , Publisher 2003, Adobe Photoshop CS.

First published in Great Britain by Fortean Words

Fortean Words
Myrtle Cottage
Woolsery
Bideford
North Devon
EX39 5QR

ISBN: 978-1-905723-60-7

To my Mountain Girl, at last....

CONTENTS

Thanks!

Many people have been of assistance to me in researching the Berwyn Mountain events. Special thanks to the following people: Geoff Richardson, Dave Clarke, David Simpson, Roger Hutchinson, Gaynor Roberts, Kyle Trotter, Scott Felton, Roger Mussom, Nick Redfern, Christine Walker, Jenny Randles, Pat Evans, Huw Lloyd, Mandy White, Ron Maddison

Acronyms

IGS: International Geological Survey (which later became)
BGS: British Geological Survey
VMRT: RAF Valley Mountain rescue Team
TA: Territorial Army
MIL: Gwynedd Constabulary's Major Incident Log
MOD: Ministry of Defence
UFO: Unidentified Flying Object (synonymous with Flying Saucer)

Maps

All grid references are based on the Llangollen & Berwyn Ordnance Survey Explorer 255 (1:25000) map

The interested reader can see all locations mentioned in this book by using Google Earth and Street View. The landscape of the Berwyn Mountains is complex and UFO researchers have differing opinions about the terminology used to denote where events took place i.e. what some believe is on the slopes of Cader Berwyn can equally be said to be on the slopes of Cader Bronwen etc. I have used the terms used by local witnesses, police and mountain rescue teams. Close study of the relevant map will clarify matters.

Documents

Some of the documents reproduced in this book have deteriorated over time and are old and basically illegible. We have included them for historical verisimilitude only.

Once Upon a Time in the West
Foreword by David Clarke

"...the central motif of the [crashed saucer legend] is that a malevolent monster (the government) has sequestered an item essential to humankind (wisdom of transcendental nature, i.e. evidence-based knowledge that we are not alone in the universe). The culture hero (the ufologist) circumvents the monster and (by investigatory prowess) releases the essential item (wisdom) for humankind..."

Charles Ziegler, anthropologist (1997)

In 1984 Jan Harold Brunvand identified what he called 'the secret truth' or crashed saucer rumour as a new category of modern legend in his classic study, *The Choking Doberman*. There are many versions of the Roswell legend but the basic outline claims a flying saucer from outer space crashed in the New Mexico desert in 1947. Wreckage from the craft and the bodies of its humanoid pilots were removed by the military and hidden in a secret hanger. Those who witnessed the operation were either sworn to secrecy or had their lives threatened. A fake cover story, suggesting the object was simply a weather balloon, was put out by the US Government who have, successfully for more than six decades, concealed the fact that "we are not alone in the universe."

Brunvand listed this story alongside other 'urban legends' he collected, such as stories about cats in microwaves and alligators in the sewers, and predicted he would get "some angry mail for suggesting this might be an area of modern legend." Such popularly-held beliefs are often dismissed by the media as "myths". This usage of myth, to indicate that something is by definition false, is misleading and incorrect. Myth is defined by the Oxford English Dictionary as "a traditional narrative sometimes popularly regarded as historical but unauthenticated". Examples include the Greek and Norse myths and the creation stories found in ancient Babylonia and the book of Genesis. Recent opinion polls have revealed that a third of Americans, and a similar number of Britons, believe that "extraterrestrial beings have visited earth at some point in the past" (Gallup 2001). Therefore it cannot be disputed that belief in alien visitors having visited earth – either at Roswell, or in ancient times - is a modern myth, as by definition it is a story or narrative which millions of people accept despite the conspicuous lack of proof.

On the other hand a legend is simply a story told about a real person, object or place that exists, existed or is believed to exist. The legend of Robin Hood is one good example. Even when a story concerns a supernatural event or person, for example UFO occupants, the legend is told as if it was true and is usually interpreted as true by those reading or listening to the story-teller. Odd as it may sound, a number of crashed saucer legends are founded upon real historical events. At Roswell no one, including the US Air Force, disputes the fact that something landed or crashed in the desert and was retrieved by the military. The USAF say that object was most probably a classified Mogul balloon, designed to spy on Soviet nuclear tests. Many (but my no means all) UFOlogists believe the object was a craft from another world containing alien pilots and, because their version is more exciting and has more emotional impact than the official version, it has attained legendary status within the wider UFO myth. In the case of the Berwyn Mountains incident that is the focus of this book, there can be no dispute that a loud explosion was heard and people saw lights in the sky. But when those basic facts diverge into stories of crashed saucers, Men in Black and conspiracies to hide 'the truth' we are once again in the realm of myth and legend.

Today, legends circulate faster than they did in the past because they have migrated from 'word of mouth' onto the internet and into books, newspapers and TV. When legends are published or circulated they are transformed by their narrators – in this case UFOlogists and journalists – in the latent process of telling and retelling. During this process some details are dropped and new information is added in order to remove contradictions so the narrators can "tell a good story". When stories are told as true they often provoke action and behaviour. This can take the form of heated debate between "believers" and sceptics who debunk the legend. Others wish to personally "live the legend" by proclaiming their own personal experiences with UFOs and aliens as confirmation of the story they believe is true.

These stories grow as part of a dynamic process, with new accounts from 'witnesses' feeding back into oral tradition to create an evolving legend. By this process stories are transformed into narrative and narrative becomes "fact" that can be experienced by others who become part of the legend. News of UFOs and UFO crashes spreads like a virus and provokes copycat behaviour, leading people in some cases to come forward with new versions or variations of the original story. In the case of Roswell a number of apparently credible people have claimed they were personally involved in the examination and movement of the wreckage and bodies from the flying saucer. Many of the stories recounted in

books such as Tom Carey and Don Schmitt's *Witness to Roswell* (2007) have been exposed as having no basis in fact. Nevertheless they continue to circulate as personal experience narratives believed both by the story-tellers and audience as true – taking us full circle.

The Berwyn Mountains incident is just one of the rapidly multiplying versions of Brunvand's suppressed truth legend. With Berwyn, as with Roswell, this consists of two distinct and divergent themes: firstly the evolving legend, told as true and believed by many and secondly, the few certain facts. Now sit back and enjoy the ride as Andy Robert's thorough investigation unpicks the strands of myth and legend to throw new light on what happened one dark January night on that dark Welsh hillside.....

Dr David Clarke
Sheffield Hallam University, July 2010

"In the end it is the mystery that lasts and not the explanation"

Sacheverell Sitwell

CHAPTER ONE

MYSTERY UPON MYSTERY

*"I've heard a lot of talk down in the village this afternoon
about a strange disc-like object which some shepherds
go as far as saying actually landed somewhere up on the
Berwyns."*

Those words were written by the science fiction writer and UFO investigator, Gavin Gibbons, in his 1958 children's science-fiction novel *By Space Ship to the Moon*, which featured a UFO landing on Moel Sych in the Berwyn Mountains of North Wales. Sixteen years later, in a surreal case of life imitating art, those very same mountains would again be the focus for a story involving a downed UFO. But this time, some said, the story was for real.

The Berwyn Mountain UFO Crash, as the event has become known by the media and by ufologists (those who study UFOs), took place over several hours on the night of 23 January 1974. The event caused widespread public panic across hundreds of square miles and attracted enormous media and public interest. The unusual events were not immediately attributed to or connected with UFOs, but were nonetheless regarded as mysterious and unsettling by those who experienced them.

Wherever mystery exists, it is human nature to seek an explanation. Within months, rumour began to circulate that a UFO may have been involved in at least some of the events of that winter's evening. As months flowed into years, a story – a legend - was forged to 'explain' the disparate events.

It was simple; UFOs had been seen in the sky, a huge explosion was heard, 'fires' and 'lights' had been seen above the village of Llandrillo, an impeccable witness had seen 'something' on the mountainside, police, RAF and soldiers were searching the area and 'men in black' were asking odd questions in the area. If even a few of the elements of the legend, which I describe in the next chapter, are true then a remarkable event or series of events took place in and around the Berwyn Mountains, a story which has never yet been satisfactorily explained.

Mysteries of any kind attract those who would seek to unravel them and soon ufologists began to take an interest in the Berwyn events. Some believed that the matrix of ostensibly separate elements were in fact connected and what lay at the root of that connection was that a UFO had crashed or landed on the Berwyn Mountains. This story took root and since the 1970s has developed to the point where an internet search on "Berwyn Mountain UFO" will yield almost 100,000 websites dealing with the subject, each based on the core elements of the event, each with its own unique interpretation of what might have caused them. Opinion and belief is firmly polarised between those who claim absolutely nothing of interest happened and those who are equally convinced that an extraterrestrial craft, a UFO, either crashed or landed in the mountains.

Since January 1974, hundreds of newspaper and magazine articles and features have been written about the Berwyn Mountain UFO Legend. It has had radio programs devoted to it and several TV documentaries have examined the mystery. UFO researchers have also taken a keen interest in what took place and it has been widely featured in UFO books and magazines. Yet despite this interest, no one has yet come up with an explanation that encompasses each element of the events of 23 January 1974.

I first became interested in the Berwyn events in 1989, when co-writing my first UFO book, (with Dr David Clarke), *Phantoms of the Sky*. Dave had written one of the more perceptive articles on the case in *UFO Brigantia*, a UFO magazine I edited. Dave expounded the theory that at least some of the Berwyn 'UFOs' might have been 'earthlights', luminescence caused by tectonic stress generated during an earthquake. Dave's theory piqued my interest in the case and from 1998 onwards, I undertook a reinvestigation of the case in attempt to find the underlying cause of what really took place and how the events became a UFO story.

The term UFO, an acronym for Unidentified Flying Object, simply means something seen in the sky that is not immediately identified. In popular culture, the acronym UFO has, however, become synonymous with the term 'flying saucer' and is taken to mean spaceships piloted by extraterrestrials. The Berwyn Mountain events are now, besides a legend, a UFO case and a UFO investigation.

A UFO investigation is a curious thing. Many people claim to be UFO investigators simply by having an interest in the subject, by reading books on the subject or perusing UFO websites. Others might have done a few basic field investigations, interviewing witnesses and tried to work out what they saw. Most people soon find out that UFO investigation is a thankless task. Even when a UFO is quickly and positively identified - as over 95% are - as the misperception of a plane, meteorological or astronomical phenomenon, a Chinese Lantern or some other mundane object, the witness is unlikely to accept the identification. The ufological literature is full of cases where the witness saw or photographed what they believed to be metallic craft of unknown origin, often performing impossible aerial manoeuvres.

Despite the vast majority of these UFOs being satisfactorily explained, the witness refrain is often steadfastly, and rightly that, "I know what I saw". Neither I nor any other serious UFO investigator believes a witness has lied if it is later discovered that the UFO had a mundane cause. However, the witnesses experience is predicated on how they perceived the event based on the information available to their senses at the time. This is coupled with a variety of other pre and post event factors; the witness's underlying beliefs about UFOs, what they have read about UFOs, how their sighting is interpreted by friends, the media and UFO investigators.

A further problem is caused by UFO investigators themselves. If, for instance an investigator holds the belief that Earth is being visited by extraterrestrials then this interpretation of the phenomena could easily influence and limit their investigation to the extent whereby they might favour evidence that supports their own personal belief and minimise that which negates it. Conversely, those investigators who believe we are not and never have been visited by extraterrestrials might choose to ignore or play down hard to explain evidence to avoid leaving a UFO case unexplained.

But adherence to either of these standpoints does not alter physical reality and as of the date of this book's publication, there is no scientific evidence that extraterrestrials exist or that Earth has been visited by them. Certainly, there are still unresolved UFO cases that, to some, might *suggest* that possibility, such as the highly contentious Roswell Incident, but the history of UFO studies demonstrates that, if enough information is available to investigators, a UFO case can usually be explained.

So, where does that leave us in the pursuit of a resolution to the Berwyn Mountain UFO Crash? Well, my personal belief is that after over thirty years as an active UFO investigator and researcher, and after publishing several books on the subject, I have seen no evidence which suggests to me that extraterrestrials are visiting or have ever visited Earth. Fortunately, whatever I or anyone else believes won't affect either whether extraterrestrials exist, *or* if they are visiting Earth so the only correct position to take must be one of agnosticism about the possibility. Although UFOs, flying saucers, and extraterrestrials, are often ridiculed in the mainstream media, the implications of their physical existence for humanity are monumental.

Imagine for a moment the consequences if aliens had fallen to earth that night in January 1974. If this *were* a proven fact, the implications are paradigm shattering. Humanity would finally know we were not alone in the universe. This revelation would be the most momentous and significant discovery in the history of the world, having a devastating effect on all our scientific, social and religious systems.

Although it would then be irrelevant, such proof would also prove that various major world governments had been keeping 'The Greatest Story Never Told' hidden from us. There would be potential for widespread social panic and the stability of political administrations would be threatened. Far from being the frivolous fancy which is portrayed by the media, and theorised by science, the possibility of actual extraterrestrial visitation is highly potent and charged with meaning and implication.

But if it *can* be demonstrated that there was no UFO, meaning no alien craft, involved in the

Berwyn events, then what kind of reality lies behind the witness experience and the popular belief? Could it have been the crash of a secret military craft such as one of the so-called 'flying triangles'? Or perhaps a failed missile test from the military rocketry ranges at nearby Aberporth? A hoax? Natural phenomena? Or something far more sinister? And if it is any, or a combination of these elements, why then have the claims of UFOs, alien cadavers and military cover-ups persisted for over three decades?

The Berwyn Incident, far from proven, is a whirling kaleidoscope of rumour, speculation and fact concerning - amongst other things - a melange of crashed UFOs, alien bodies, military retrieval teams, earth tremors, meteorites, weapons testing, disinformation agents, Men in Black and geologically created lights.

Any discussion of a UFO case has to rely on evidence. But what is admissible as evidence? Can we believe something just because one or two people saw it? Can we believe what they described was actually what they saw? Rationalists would have us believe that all experience can be explained by science; yet the abundance and variety of supernatural and religious belief found throughout history and across the world indicates that mystery does exist and cannot always be reduced to easily understood 'facts'. We would do well to bear in mind Sherlock Holmes' observation that when you have eliminated the impossible, whatever remains, *however improbable*, must be the truth.

In sifting through all the evidence for (and against) the Berwyn Mountain UFO Crash, in an attempt to eliminate the impossible and to arrive, hopefully, at the truth of what took place, I have been reliant on many sources of information. In the search for accuracy, I have clearly identified what is speculation, what is probability and what is known fact. I have used only verifiable information drawn - where possible - from primary and secondary sources, and have attempted to cross reference those sources to validate each particular aspect of the case and to follow the 'paper trail' where it leads.

It is the concept of the paper trail that is the most important element of this investigation. If a genuine UFO in the sense of a piloted, structured craft of extraterrestrial origin crashed (or landed as some have it) in the Berwyn Mountains and if that craft was known about or even retrieved by the military as is claimed, then there must be at least *some* evidence. Documents somewhere must - however obliquely - refer to some aspect of the event, whether it is military or police documents or corroborative interviews with witnesses, and since 1998, I have been fortunate in having had unique access to a wide variety of documents and witness statements which have informed my investigation of the case.

On the other hand, if there was no UFO, if one follows the same paper trail, it should really be possible to untangle the elements that gave rise to the myth that a UFO came to ground and to arrive at a satisfactory resolution to the mystery.

This may be a short book but it is complex, and the reader will not be able to pick it up and flick through it to find easy answers. The book needs to be read as a whole, for a number of reasons. Because the Berwyn Mountain events were not immediately thought of as a UFO case, it is functionally impossible to tell the story from the beginning. Instead, I have summed up the *legend* that it has become, and then attempted to unravel the legend in order to make sense of it. You will find that some information is repeated several times. This is intentional, as the information needs to be seen from different perspectives, and rotated like a Rubik's Cube until it begins to form a cohesive and interlocking account in which each part of the story makes sense when set against others.

My own views about the Berwyn Mountain UFO Crash have changed over the years. I have modified my theories as new pieces of evidence have become known and in at least one part of the case have had to revise it completely. My investigation has been a journey deep into the heart of a complex modern mystery, into what people believe and on what basis they hold that belief. And where I thought there was no mystery I found, to my surprise, that there actually was. Frustrating and revelatory by turns, researching and writing this book has been a journey of illumination. I hope it is for you too.

CHAPTER TWO

THE LEGEND OF THE BERWYN MOUNTAIN UFO CRASH

Aliens crash riddle would baffle Scully and Mulder
Daily Star, 9 September 1996

T he 'choppers' had been seen for some time across northern Britain, unidentified helicopters, flying over the uplands of Yorkshire, Lancashire, Cheshire, Derbyshire and north Wales. They were seen flying low across treacherous terrain and in every kind of weather. And they baffled the authorities. Private helicopters were rare in the early 1970s and the police and airfields could account for all of them. But not the 'Phantom Helicopters', as these mystery craft were dubbed by the press. They were different. Illuminated with odd colours, and carrying unusual light configurations they were seen at all hours of day and night.

If they had a purpose, it was hidden to both the public who observed them and to the police who hunted them. IRA terrorists? Drug smugglers? Illegal immigrants? These and many other theories were bandied around, but no concrete evidence was forthcoming to support any of them. And still they flew.

The phantom flyers were seen several times in late January in Cheshire and Staffordshire, near the border between England and Wales. Those who saw them said they seemed to be looking for something. What this 'something' was would soon become clear just a few days later. They were looking for - perhaps expecting - an unidentified flying object. They would find one soon enough.

Meanwhile, as the phantom 'copters flitted across the night skies, a troop of soldiers had been briefed with an unusual mission. They were ordered to travel north from their headquarters and await further instructions. No further information was given to them. They too would soon find what they didn't even know they were looking for.

OH, WHAT A NIGHT!

Wednesday the 23rd of January 1974 was just another winter's day in Bala and the nearby villages of Llandrillo and Llandderfel. The weather was cold and wet with patches of snow clinging to the nearby Berwyn Mountains. UFOs were the very last thing on the minds of the villagers engaged in their everyday business. But as darkness closed in a series of events took place that was to change all that and which had far-reaching effects; effects which are still being discussed in the area over thirty-five years later.

Shortly after 8.30 p.m., people in the Bala area were jolted from their evening activities by a terrible rumbling noise lasting four or five seconds. This was followed almost immediately by the sound of a massive explosion. Furniture moved, ornaments and pictures fell from walls and shelves, buildings shook and livestock voiced their terror into the night. Thousands of terrified people shot to their windows to scan the night skies, before flooding into the streets in an attempt to discover the cause of the disturbance.

Many of those jolted into activity by the disturbance vividly recall a huge white and green light streaking across the heavens. Others saw a brilliant flash of light and some said a fire could be seen on the mountain. As these lights died away, looking toward the mountains, bright fingers of light probing vertically into the night sky could clearly be seen.

Police phone lines quickly became jammed as hundreds of terrified people tried to contact the emergency services. Of those people, one, a nurse, was convinced that the noise was that of an aircraft crashing on the Berwyn Mountains. She eventually got through to the police and told them she was going to drive up the mountain road in advance of any emergency services, to offer first aid to any survivors. And so, loading her two small daughters into her car, she set off into the miserable winter's night, a night that would change her life forever.

The nurse drove quickly and confidently over roads she knew well, keen to get to the site of what she believed was an air disaster. As she drove, she scanned the black mountains ahead for any signs of light as she made her way onto the tops. Once she reached the summit of the deserted mountain road she halted, astonished at what she could see before her. There, high on the barren mountainside was a huge, glowing ball of light.

Whatever the object was it was too far from the road to be reached on foot. She and her daughters watched, flabbergasted as the ball of light slowly pulsated, changing colour from red to yellow to white and back again. It was strange. There were no flames and whatever it was didn't look like what she would have expected an air disaster to resemble. The nurse and her daughters could only stare, mystified at the scene before them.

As she viewed this astonishing sight, the nurse could see other lights. Some were small, like torches, and others were like those of a vehicle. They were moving round and toward the huge light on the hillside. Baffled, unable to identify what she was looking at and realising she was too far away to be of any practical assistance the nurse set off for home.

On the journey back down the mountain road to her village she saw more vehicles ahead and was surprised to be flagged down and stopped by a group of police and soldiers. They were clearly unhappy at seeing her there and forcefully ordered her off the mountain, telling her the road was now cordoned off and all members of the public were banned from it.

At about the same time, another local family were determined to find the underlying cause of the lights and massive explosion. They drove from their home in Llandrillo up the forestry road that led from the village on to the slopes of Cader Bronwen. As they neared the end of the narrow track through the woods, they and other locals who were trying to find out what was going on, were also halted by police and turned back. As they reversed, they caught a glimpse through the trees of a huge pinky-red pulsating object. Clearly, the nurse wasn't the only person to have seen something odd.

Official reaction was quick to the explosion. Suspiciously quick said some people. Police and military personnel appeared as if from nowhere, arriving in the area within minutes, turning the curious villagers away from all access roads to the mountains. A party of unknown police officers, guided by a local farmer's son, drove up onto the remote hillside but could initially see nothing. Then, just before they set off back to the valley, a light appeared above them which lit up the landscape as though it were day, being seen from miles around. As quickly as it appeared, it vanished and darkness descended once again on the mysterious mountains.

STARS, AND RUMOURS OF STARS

In the days following, a large military presence appeared in the area. Roads remained closed and farmers complained they were forbidden from tending their stock due to large areas of the mountain being cordoned off. Clearly, it seems that something was being sought. Or why else would military helicopters and aircraft be criss-crossing the area and strangers methodically combing the mountainsides? More suspicious still were the dark-suited officials who arrived in the area, going door to door, and asking a series of odd questions about the recent events on the mountain.

A few days after the incident, a group of people were in the area, carrying out a survey of a stone circle which stood on the slopes of one of the Berwyn Mountains. Their instruments recorded unusually high radiation readings at the stones, readings that could not be accounted for. Were these readings, they mused, connected in some strange way with the events a few days earlier on the same mountains?

Whatever caused the noise and lights attracted serious TV and radio coverage. National and regional papers, including *The Guardian* and *The Times* all carried detailed reports of the events. Speculation was rife but inconclusive. An aircraft crash would have accounted for the noise, lights and official involvement. But no crash site was ever identified. Yet one local newspaper was certain that the event involved a crash of some kind, noting:

"There is a report that an Army vehicle was seen coming down the mountain near Bala Lake with a large square box on the back of it and accompanied by outriders."

Despite the rumours, the authorities refused to acknowledge that anything unusual had taken place at all. The police claimed they could not find any cause for the mystery noise and lights and categorically stated there had been no crash. Scientists and knowledgeable members of the public suggested that meteors and earth tremors were responsible for the noise and lights. But what could possibly explain the glowing sphere seen by the nurse, the huge flash of light and the beams of light seen on the mountain by hundreds of people?

These phenomena were swiftly dismissed by armchair pundits as the villagers' imaginations, shooting stars, or more ludicrously as people out poaching hares. Such natural phenomenon was also unlikely to lead to roads or large areas of mountainside being closed by the army. There was no consistency to the stories; nothing added up. Local people weren't fools. They were there. They experienced the events. They *knew* something out of the ordinary had taken place, they just didn't know what. The media soon forgot about the incident and the locals too let the matter fade deep into their memories. But UFO researchers realised that something had occurred that had not been at all satisfactorily explained. Lights in the sky, and mysterious explosions, coupled with unusual military activity are avidly noted by the UFO community as indicators of a UFO crash. Various UFO journals reported the events but no investigation was undertaken and no real conclusions were offered. The mystery prevailed.

SECRETS AND LIES?

But shadowy forces were at work. Within a year of the actual event, UFO investigators began to receive official-looking documents from a top-secret group claiming to be called Aerial Phenomena Enquiry Network (APEN). These papers made the staggering claim that an extra-terrestrial craft had come down on the Berwyn Mountains, and had been retrieved for study by an APEN crash retrieval team! Furthermore, APEN also claimed there had been a key witness to the UFO crash who they were recommending for hypnotic regression.

The APEN documents led to greater interest in the events and by the late 1970s, ufologists had begun to investigate the Berwyn incident. One of Britain's most famous UFO researchers, Jenny Randles, was a frequent holiday visitor to the region and recalled the locals discussing military activity on the mountains in the wake of some crash-like event. These tales of a UFO intrigued Jenny and she started to make enquiries, trying to untangle the fact from the fiction, certain that *something* unusual had taken place in the Berwyn Mountains that January night in 1974.

In 1984, while giving a talk about UFOs at RAF Shawbury, Jenny raised the subject of the events in the Berwyn Mountains and "there was an awkward silence from senior personnel". Jenny initially wrote that the Berwyn events could have been caused by naturally occurring 'earthlights' or perhaps because of a military accident involving nuclear material.

The nuclear radiation theory tied in nicely with the readings taken at the stone circle less than a week after the event. Further evidence of radiation was introduced to the legend in 1995 when Jenny Randles was approached by a science correspondence from a national newspaper. He told of being sent by his editor to the Bala area (only a few miles from Llandrillo and Llanderfel) to look into a 'hot spot' of childhood leukaemia cases. Initial speculation that the nuclear plant at Trawsfynedd was responsible proved negative. Could the Berwyn event have involved a lost nuclear warhead? Or, perhaps, radiation leaking from a crashed UFO? These theories were food for thought and sustenance for rumour. Ufologists recalled the infamous Roswell Incident from America in 1947. Was Berwyn the UK's equivalent?

A breakthrough came in 1996, when a former soldier broke his silence to speak to ufologists. He told how the military knew in advance that a UFO was going to come down on the Berwyn Mountains but didn't know exactly when. Helicopters had been sent to search for the craft. He and his fellow soldiers were sent north to Wales where they were eventually sent to Llandrillo. There they met another group of soldiers who gave them a box with instructions to take it to the top-secret biological warfare establishment of Porton Down in Wiltshire. Once there the boxes were opened and the soldier was shocked to see alien bodies and even more shocked to be informed that at least one alien had been captured alive. Sworn to secrecy the soldier kept quiet, in fear of his very life and his pension. But the immensity of what he had seen, and its implications for humanity preyed on his conscience and he eventually felt he could keep silent no longer. Other ex-soldiers started to contact ufologists and hinted at *their* involvement in the retrieval of an extraterrestrial craft. What had been secret for so long was now out in the open.

COVER UP CONSPIRACY

UFO researchers now turned their attentions to the Berwyn UFO in earnest. Now, the Berwyn Mountain events were Britain's equivalent to the infamous Roswell UFO crash of 1947 and they were going to prove, finally, that a UFO had been removed by the military. They had the information and the witnesses; all they needed now was the evidence. But, it seemed, every angle of research was closed off to them. The Ministry of Defence denied having a file on the incident and police records from 1974 had allegedly long since been destroyed. Some investigators suspected a cover up. This seemed to be confirmed by the government infiltrators that some elements in the UFO community claimed were in their midst. These people were claiming to be ufologists who had resolved the Berwyn case as being nothing more than a series of misperceptions. Rumour had it that they had been placed in the UFO community by MI5 to spread disinformation, to rubbish the very idea that a UFO could have crashed in the Berwyn Mountains.

Television and radio documentaries were made about the Berwyn Mountain UFO. But, said some UFO researchers, it was always the MI5 infiltrators who appeared to pour scepticism on any claim that alien craft were involved. UFO researchers who *knew* about the crashed UFO were often filmed but their contributions were left on the cutting room floor, on the orders of the secret intelligence services. This then is the Legend of the Berwyn Mountain UFO. It is time now to examine the facts to see what truth, if any lies at the heart of the legend.

CHAPTER THREE

A BERWYN MOUNTAIN MYSTERIOGRAPHY

*"Not with the best of gay companions would I hike over the Berwyns at night
when the wind is high and the rain hisses from the tops of the rocky places"*
Cledwyn Hughes

The UFO phenomenon in general and the Berwyn Mountain UFO case in particular begs many questions. Not least, where do UFOs crash? Well, they certainly never crash in towns and cities, on motorways or, in fact, anywhere with a high population density. It would be impossible, for instance, for the government to cover up the crash of an extraterrestrial craft on the sea front at Rhyl!

But the legend of the Berwyn Mountain UFO crash is a mystery and, whether fact or fiction, mystery requires a geographical location. In this instance, it is the area known as the Berwyn Mountains of North Wales. To understand the events that comprise the Berwyn Mountain UFO legend it is first useful to get an idea of their geographical location, and to set the UFO story in context with other mysteries from the area.

The Berwyn range runs roughly east west, stretching from the border of Wales with Shropshire to the eastern boundaries of Snowdonia. The A5 trunk road from London to Holyhead runs below their northern slopes, most travellers barely giving the mountains a second glance as they head to the tourist honey-pots of Snowdonia. Little do they know they are driving past a remarkable, atmospheric and seldom visited wilderness. In his classic Welsh travelogue of 1862, *Wild Wales*, George Borrow followed the Victorian trend for romanticising mountain landscapes and described the Berwyns as "darkly blue, a rain cloud like ink, hanging over their summits. Oh, the wild hills of Wales, the land of old renown and of wonder, the land of Arthur and Merlin".

Opinion is divided as to how the Berwyn Mountains got their name. Welsh scholar T. Gwynn Jones believed that Berwyn might have its origins in fairy folklore, being a mutation of Bryn (iau) Gwyn (ap Nudd), the Welsh word for hill, bryn, having mutated to Bre, giving us Bre Gwyn which, over the course of time had become Berwyn. Less fanciful sources suggest the word comes from the much more straightforward marrying of barr, meaning head and wyn, meaning white; white head referring to the snow which often caps the peaks well into April. The mountain range consists of several named peaks, the main ones being Cadair Bronwen (785m), Cadair Berwyn (830m) and Moel Sych (827m). Although far from being the highest mountains in Wales their terrain can be dangerous for the unprepared or unwary. Mountain rescue teams have frequently been called out to the area in order to rescue lost, injured or dead walkers. The mountain peaks are frequently cloaked in mist or low cloud, proving a hazard to aircraft. At least six military or civilian 'planes have crashed into the Berwyn Mountains since the 1930s, resulting in the loss of several lives. In winter conditions, the area transforms into remote and difficult terrain, an ideal spot if ever there was one, for UFO activity.

Only one road bisects the Berwyns. This is the B4391 Milltir Cerrig (Rocky Mile) mountain pass road, which rises to the not insignificant height of 486 metres and runs roughly north to south, from Llandderfel to Llangynog. As you will see in Chapter 5, the experiences of one individual on this road are central to the Berwyn Mountain UFO story.

Wildlife thrives on the heather covered mountain slopes. Birds of prey such as Hen Harrier, Merlin, Peregrine Falcons, and Buzzards hunt there, while Snipe, Curlew, Raven and Short Eared Owls are also seen. The moorland and forested areas provide a safe habitat for creatures such as rabbits and polecats and rare plants abound, including the mountain blackberry.

Population density on the mountains is virtually zero; there are no villages on the mountains but isolated farms and houses are to be found down in the valleys and on the lower slopes. Immediately beneath the northern slopes of the range lie the small villages of Llandrillo and Llandderfel, both of which played a central role in the events of January 23 1974, while the market town of Bala is situated a few kilometres to the northeast.

People have lived and worshipped here since early prehistoric times, leaving a dramatic ritual landscape to which many beliefs have become attached and in which many mysteries other than UFOs dwell. The mountaintops themselves have been the focus of human activity for millennia. Cadair Bronwen (Bronwen's Chair) has on its summit a prehistoric burial cairn called Bwrdd Arthur (Arthur's Table). In 1773, the Welsh naturalist and antiquary Thomas Pennant wrote:

> "The vast Berwyn Mountains are the eastern boundary of this beautiful vale. Their highest tops are Cader Frenwen and Cader Ferwen. On the first is a great heap of stones brought from some distant part, with great toil, up the steep ascent; and in their middle is en erect pillar. Of him, whose ambition climbed this height for a monument, we are left in ignorance."

Sadly, the pillar has long since gone and the cairn is now eroded to small pile of stones. The moors and mountain slopes are strewn with numerous prehistoric remains. On the moorland above the waterfall, sweeping upwards toward Moel Sych, is Rhos y Beddau, the moor of the graves, on which can be found stone circles, standing stones and burial mounds; providing mute testimony to the reverence accorded to this landscape by its former inhabitants. On the south side of the Berwyns, the numinous waterfall Pistyll Rhaeadr is host to legends relating to two giants and their doomed attempts to build a house beneath the falls. To the north of the range, the lower slopes of Cadair Bronwen play host to Moel ty Uchaf, a small stone circle situated in a commanding position giving breathtaking panoramic and dramatic views along the Dee Valley. This megalith plays a small but significant role in the Berwyn Mountain UFO legend.

Folklore records these peaks have been haunted by a multitude of aerial phenomena over the centuries and some contemporary paranormal puzzles still abound. Unusual lights have been observed dancing on and around the mountain summits and in the deep valleys and in the 20th century there were many sightings of a "phantom" World War Two bomber, perhaps the ghost of one of the numerous Berwyn Mountain aircraft disasters. Other supernatural denizens sighted in the area include "Teggie", Llyn Tegid's lake monster, and dozens of so-called "alien big cats"; puma like creatures that are often seen but never caught, either on film or in traps.

Besides the many old legends attached to the Berwyn Mountains there are modern mysteries too, one of which was possibly UFO related. A 1975 issue of *Flying Saucer Review* featured an article titled *The Army and E.M. Effects* that related the story of an unnamed soldier serving in a reserve unit. He and at least thirty over soldiers were sent to an area near Lake Bala on the instructions of RAF Valley (Anglesey), who sent information that an aircraft had crashed in a remote valley.

A search was undertaken during which several vehicles stalled and would not re-start, which resulted in the soldiers being ordered to advance on foot. But once they had advanced past the line of stalled vehicles, they lost their willpower and each one reported being affected by "mental interference". This happened several times and eventually the search was abandoned. Later that day, as the soldiers were eating their evening meal, they heard an odd humming noise and the reflection of a bright yellow-orange light could be seen in the valley they had attempted to search. A number of the soldiers believed this was a flying saucer and were afraid. Yet another attempt was made to search the valley but once more the vehicles stalled and the troops were once again repelled by the "mental interference".

The puzzling story ends with the soldier's unit being stood down and another unit moving in. In 1980, 16 years after the Berwyn events, a radio transmitter described as being "of foreign origin" was discovered by a farmer ploughing his field at Llanrhaeadr-y-Mochnant, on the southern side of the Berwyns. The riddle of who buried it or why they did was never solved, but it was speculated that the sophisticated transmitter was hidden by a party of Russians who stayed in the area during 1971.

Old legends and modern mysteries, all inextricably intertwined with the wild and virtually trackless mountains. If the Berwyn Mountain UFO is supernatural in nature, just one of a long line of anomalous phenomena witnessed in those hills, it could not have chosen a better place to appear. If it was a physical alien craft then it was fortunate to have come to earth in such a remote area that provided concealment from the public and also cover for the military crash retrieval team to remove it. It is against this mysteriographical backdrop that on 23 January 1974 the Berwyn Mountain UFO legend began.

What you are about to read next is a composite account of the Berwyn Mountain UFO crash legend. I have merged into one story the myriad and disparate elements of the Berwyn legend, drawn from books, magazine and newspaper articles, TV and radio documentaries and internet sources. This is the popular legend of the Berwyn Mountain UFO crash. It is now time to tell that legend, before examining its component parts in microscopic detail.

CHAPTER FOUR
ARE YOU READY TO RUMBLE?
January 23, 1974
8.38 p.m.

"It was serious enough to get all the drinkers out of the local pub!"
Police Sergeant Elfed Roberts, 2008

The initial, core event in the Berwyn Mountain UFO event took place at 8.38 p.m. on 23 January 1974. How we can be so precise about the time will become clear as the story develops. The times given by those who witnessed the event however are more an artefact of memory, and as such range from between 7.55 p.m. and midnight. Everyone who witnessed the event has his or her own memories of the core event, from the mundane to the dramatic. The crucial point is that all elements of the Berwyn Mountain UFO legend stem from this one event and as such, the experiences of those involved repay careful study.

In this chapter, I have attempted to piece together the experiences and reactions of a number of people who were involved in the Berwyn events, from those who lived in the Llandrillo area, to those living further afield through to the police and other emergency services. I have taken these accounts of the event from a variety of primary sources including personal statements, police and RAF files as well as from TV, radio and print media.

Many people who experienced the event at 8.38 p.m. have used the words "tremor", "rumble" and "explosion", among other adjectives, to describe what they felt. For consistency, I have used the term "tremor" for events throughout the chapter.

The early 1970s found Britain, and thus Wales, in the depths of political turmoil. Inflation was running at 17%, which had caused a pay freeze. This in turn caused conflict with the powerful trade unions of the time, resulting in the National Union of Mineworkers - later to be smashed by the Thatcher government - bringing in a 'work to rule'. Prime Minister Edward Heath, in an attempt to conserve coal stocks, introduced the 3-day week, only allowing the commercial use of electricity three days of out of each week. Austere times were the backdrop against which something very odd was to happen in the Berwyn Mountains.

January 23, 1974 was a typically cold winter's day in Llandrillo, although there was only a thin covering of snow on the high tops. By 8.38 p.m., darkness had long since fallen and the weather was now windy with partial cloud cover at high altitude and patches of scattered low cloud. Rain fell intermittently throughout the evening, ranging from a light drizzle to heavy downpours.

I, WITNESS

Police Sergeant Elfed Roberts had just come off duty when:

> "All of a sudden I felt this ominous rumbling sound and clearly something quite major had happened. My first thoughts were oh, heavens it's the dam above the town of Bala that's gone." [i]

Roberts set off immediately for Bala and we will pick his story up in a later chapter.

For Mary Evans of Llechwedd Farm in Llandrillo, the event at 8.38 p.m. was, "The most frightening noise that I have ever heard." Her husband, Gwyn, ran outside but could not see anything to account for the noise.

> "Whatever created the noise it only lasted for a few minutes but there was a terrific explosion and we thought the house was going to cave in on us as the whole building felt as if it had been rocked to its foundations." [ii]

Val Walls, of Bro Dinam, in the centre of Llandrillo was also unnerved by the tremor.

> "I remember it so distinctly, it's frightening really. I'd just washed the week's milk bottles and put them on the draining board when there was a bang, a definite impact, not an explosion, a definite bang of something hitting the ground. There was a peculiar sensation following that, like if you're standing on the Underground in London with a train going beneath you, it was that sort of sensation, only more like a rolling sensation. It went 'thud' and then came from the left and it rolled under my feet."

The time lapse between the 'thud' and the rolling sensation was, according to Val, "Instantaneous, one or two seconds." [iii] Mary Jones, who at the time lived half way up a small mountain near Corwen had a similar experience of the event, it being like, "The sensation of a London tube train rattling beneath us." [iv]

Everyone, it seemed, had a slightly different perception of what had taken place. For Rhiannon

Evans of Llandrillo there was no 'thud'. But the plates on her dresser rattled and moved round and there was a noise, "You thought it was somehow terrifying. It seemed to be above somehow, more than under. Quite terrifying really..." [v]

FIRE ON THE MOUNTAIN?

Police Constable Owen, Llandrillo's village police officer, felt the tremor at about 8.40 p.m. He rushed to open his curtains to look over the mountains and saw a "Big bright glow in the sky over the brow of the hill", to the southeast. His initial thought was that a 'plane had crashed. The bright glow faded but, somewhat alarmed, he rushed down to the village. In Llandrillo, from the bridge over the Afon Ceidiog he looked up toward the mountains and could see two bright beams of light, like searchlights. The beams were white and were moving about in the sky, and lasted for a couple of minutes. [vi]

At 9.00 p.m., P.C. Owen made an emergency 999 call from the Llandrillo telephone box next to the bridge. His call was recorded verbatim by the Police Operations Control room over at Colwyn Bay. P.C. Owen said, "There was a terrific explosion. I heard it. There is a flashing light up on Cader Bronwen it could be a crashed aircraft." The beams of light had disappeared when Owen left the phone box, so he went to the *Dudley Arms* public house. [vii]

Several other villages saw these beams of light immediately after the 8.38 p.m. tremor. Glyn Jones went outside observed two distinct lights going up and down. Another, and unnamed, witness saw them for at least twenty minutes after the explosion and noted that they appeared to be just over the brow of the hill above Llandrillo. This witness believed it was a lamp used by poachers, who frequently hunted on the lower slopes of the Berwyn Mountains. Poachers with powerful lights were mentioned several times in witness statements with relation to the light beams seen in the sky and, as we will see, local poachers did play a key role in part of the evening's events.

Tegid Jones from Corwen wrote to me in 1998 to say:

> "I happened to be in the bedroom window that night about five to eight o' clock at night. I saw something come out of the sky. It was a big ball all red with sparks coming from it. My furniture was rattling like hell for a few seconds then it went towards Llandrillo." It is unlikely Tegid was correct in his time as the tremor did not take place until forty-three minutes later and there are no other reports linking the tremor to lights seen in the sky earlier than 8.38 p.m. [viii]

Martin Brown, a resident of Berwyn Street in Llandrillo, was an early caller. "There has been a loud explosion in the area and there is a large fire on the mountainside", he told the police. "Can you see the fire from where you are standing?" queried the operator? Brown answered, "Yes". [ix]

FIGURES

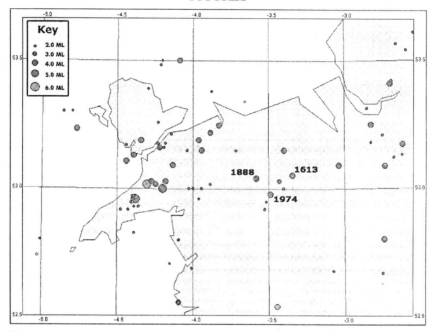

Figure 1

Seismicity of North Wales. Dates are shown for earthquakes discussed in the text.

Numbers/dates of major earthquakes in North Wales - (Roger Mussom/BGS)

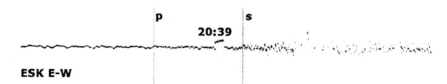

Figure 4

Example seismogram of the 23 January 1974 earthquake – the E-W horizontal component of the short-period WWSSN instrument at Eskdalemuir Observatory. Picks (p and s) are those made by G. Neilson in 1974.

The earthquake as recorded by instrumentation at the time - (Roger Mussom/BGS)

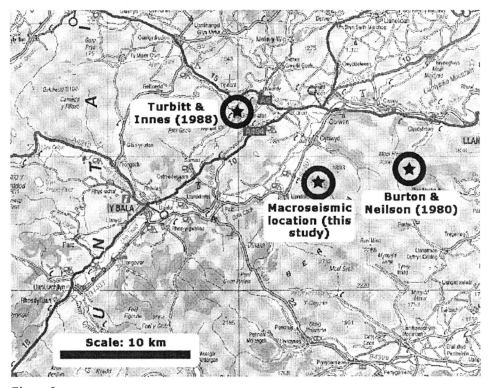

Figure 3

Location map for epicentral determinations of the 23 January 1974 earthquake.

Various estimated locations for epicentre of quake - (Roger Mussom/BGS)

Such was the volume of telephone calls that it took some people a while to get through to the police. Mr. Bisco, from Llandrillo eventually got through at 8.54 p.m. and reported:

> "There has been a tremendous explosion and I can see lights on the mountain. I think it's a crashed aircraft. My wife states there are lights flickering on the mountain."

In one of the many peculiar and unresolved speculations connected with the events that evening, Mr Bisco added:

> "My neighbour thinks it's a man made explosion. He saw a Landrover making its way up the mountain earlier this evening." [x]

A FIERY TALE?

Mrs Annie Williams and Mrs Elizabeth Hughes described what they experienced as being like "something out of *Dr Who*". On feeling the tremor, they rushed from their bungalow at Bro Dinam, Mrs Williams later telling *The Guardian*, "I saw this bright light hanging in the sky. It had a long, fiery tail, which seemed to be sparking off small stars. It seemed to be motionless for several minutes, going dim and then very brilliant, like a dormant fire which keeps coming to life. It would have been like an electric bulb in shape except it seemed to have rough edges, then fell somewhere behind the hills at the back of my bungalow and the earth shook." [xi]

In examining the numerous witness accounts there appeared to be several different sightings of lights around the time of the 8.38 p.m. tremor. A large, apparently slow moving, red/pink ball of fire, seen in the sky seconds after the tremor; a white glow, also seen immediately after the tremor; a red "fire" or "bonfire" seen immediately after the tremor and at least two beams of white light seen between 8.38 p.m. and 9.00 p.m.

An analysis of witness accounts indicates the ball of fire was travelling more or less east to west and passed over the Corwen area before disappearing over the Berwyn Mountains to the southwest. The white glows, flashes of light and fires were perceived as being high up, above the horizon as visible from Llandrillo and, according to witnesses either in the air or on the mountain itself. To fully appreciate what the villages of Llandrillo saw, the reader should refer to the map on page 31. From the village, to the east and southeast, the land rises sharply and it is not possible to see the summits of the Berwyn Mountains or even their higher slopes. To the south, and southeast, where many of the lights were observed, wooded hillsides give way to a flatter area, prior to the slopes rising to the peaks of Cader Bronwen, Cader Berwyn and Moel Sych. This means that any lights were either shining up from this flatter area, or were in the sky above the mountain range.

Due to the length of time between the events of 23 January 1974 and the investigation of the case, it is difficult to separate out the various witness accounts. As time passes people's memories have, to a certain extent, faltered. Moreover, the considerable media coverage of the

Berwyn UFO legend between 1974 and 2010 has led to memories being conflated with media reports. However, we can be certain that the aerial light seen immediately after the tremor were not local to the Llandrillo area. For example, Mrs. K Hughes, of Rhos on Sea, on the north coast of Wales, recalls aerial light phenomena at the same time as the tremor. She was at her night class at the local Technical College when she felt the earth shake and, looking out of the window she saw, "Two flaming pink balls of fire one after the other fall from the sky". [xii]

Many of the witness in Llandrillo who saw "fires" and "lights" reported they were red and round and in at least one case – listed above- like a "bonfire". This begs the question as to whether the witnesses to glows, lights and fires had all seen the aerial phenomenon, witnessed by Tegid Jones, which passed over Corwen toward Llandrillo? This could be entirely possible, as none of the witnesses in and around Llandrillo noted the "bonfire" or "fire" was there for any length of time; it seemed to be a phenomenon that was seen briefly but due to the words used- fire and bonfire- appeared to have had some permanence, however brief. Mona Scholz saw a light "like a distant fire, or sheet lightning behind the mountain." There will be a detailed analysis of what could have been responsible for these lights in later chapters. [xiii]

The tremor was felt just as strongly on southern side of the Berwyn Mountains. In hamlets such as Llanrhaeadr, Mrs. Francis Denby experienced the event as, "...a loud rumble, we thought one of the derelict barns had fallen down". [xiv] Rhys Meredith, from nearby Llangynog, observed, "... the earth shook and the floor of the house seemed to give; one's legs seemed to give beneath one" [xv]. Whatever caused the event, although it seemed strongest in the area immediately around Llandrillo, was powerful enough to be perceived many miles distant.

The tremor was reported from Ruthin, some 14 linear miles distant away, where it was so powerful that someone believed their partially built house extension had collapsed. It was also felt in Denbigh (18 miles) and Abergele (27 miles). Although it was not known on the evening of the 23rd, later reports indicated that the tremor was felt as far north as Liverpool (40), south as far as Barmouth (30 miles) in the west at Aberdaron (55 miles) and in several locations in the West Midlands (over 50 miles). Clearly, an aircraft crash would not have been felt at such distances. But during the evening of the 23rd, everything seemed local, and centred very much on Llandrillo and the mountain range that towered over the little Welsh village.

EXPLOSION

The sheer volume of telephone calls which were coming into Police stations across North Wales galvanised the police to action. At 9.00 p.m., Gwynedd Constabulary opened a Major Incident Log (MIL). The Officer in Charge was Inspector A. R. Vaughan and the nature of the incident was termed "EXPLOSION", based on that term being used by many of the callers. A Major Incident Log was the police's way of ensuring all relevant phone calls were recorded in one specific document that also gave details of the time and whom the call was from, what the purpose and content of the message was, what action was taken and any additional remarks. The MIL gives a small but valuable insight to how the police coordinated operations that night and fixes with some certainty the times of various key events. [xvi]

Phone box in Llandrillo from which the police were inundated with calls

Dudley Arms hotel- Llandrillo

It is clear from entries in the MIL that the authorities' first thoughts were that the tremor was caused by a crashed aircraft. This perception was based solely on telephone reports from members of the public describing bangs, explosions, rumblings, a sensation of impact and various lights both in the sky and on the Berwyn Mountains. Although no one had reported hearing or seeing a 'plane in distress the assumption by the police was logical and set the template for their reactions. Entries in the MIL for 9.00 p.m. indicate the Merioneth fire and ambulance services were placed on standby, as was the Wrexham ambulance service. None of the emergency services other than the police was initially sent out.

This has puzzled some people who can't understand why, if the police believed an aircraft disaster had taken place, all the relevant emergency services were not immediately rushed to the scene. This did not take place because although the police had received numerous phone calls from members of the public, and indeed their own officers, which were *suggesting* that an aircraft catastrophe had occurred, they had no actual evidence that one *had*. At 9.00 p.m., there had been no reports of missing civilian, private or military aircraft and there was no identified crash site for the emergency services to attend. In these circumstances, the police did what they could to prepare for the *possibility* of an aircraft tragedy, which was to send officers out to the Llandrillo area in order to determine what the course of action should be. [xvii]

As part of this state of readiness, at 8.56 p.m., a call was made to RAF Valley on Ynys Môn (Anglesey) to check if they were aware of any crashed aircraft. They were not, however Flight Lieutenant Strachan from the RAF Valley Mountain Rescue Team (VMRT) requested full information about the incident and confirmed he had put the Mountain Rescue Team on standby. [xviii]

At 9.45 p.m., Lancashire police phoned to confirm Air Traffic Control at Preston reported no civilian aircraft were missing. It now seemed much less likely that an air disaster had taken place. With this in mind, the police then checked with local and national military contacts to check if any exercises were taking place that could have been responsible for the tremor and lights. These enquiries were all negative.

The police also checked with Park Hall camp in Oswestry to see if any Army cadets were on exercise in the area. This also drew a negative response, the cadets being on exercise 42 miles away to the southwest at Devils' Bridge. [xix]

Sgt Oldham, of the VMRT phoned the police at 9.58 p.m. to inform them he was in Bangor on standby with Cpl Pritchard and Flight Sgt Hass. He called again at 10.22 p.m. to report he was setting off for Llandrillo and bringing a Dr. Jones with him. [xx]

The penultimate timed entry in the Major Incident Log for the 23rd January noted that the Eskdalemuir Observatory in Scotland had recorded a medium earth tremor at 8.39 p.m., which had lasted one minute. Those witnesses who had described their experience as feeling a tremor had been correct and whatever had caused the tremor was so powerful it had been recorded over 160 miles away. What had caused the tremor, however, was still a matter for conjecture. [xxi]

Between 8.38 p.m. and midnight, while the police were receiving and collating calls from the public, a number of other people in the Llandrillo area were involved in what appear to be their own small dramas connected to the events, which will be discussed in later chapters. But it was a call made to the police from the tiny village of Llandrillo that was to have far-reaching consequences for the development of the night's events into a full-blown UFO case. For Pat Evans, a District Nurse living in the tiny village of Llandderfel, just over three miles from Llandrillo, Wednesday 23 January 1974 had begun and passed without incident. Then, at 8.38 p.m., it began to turn into one of the most puzzling days of her life.

NOTES

i.   Interview with researchers for Britain's Closest Encounters , Firefly Productions, 2008
ii.   Letter to AR, 14/2/1998
iii.   Interview with AR, 20/2/1998
iv.   Letter to AR, 15/1/1998
v.   Interview with AR, 30/1/1998
vi.   Colwyn Bay Police Operations Room message, 9.00 p.m. 23/1/1974
vii.   Colwyn Bay Police Operations Room message, 9.00 p.m. 23/1/1974
viii.   Letter to AR, January 1998
ix.   Colwyn Bay Police Operations Room message, untimed, 23/1/1974
x.   Colwyn Bay Police Operations Room message, 8.54 p.m. 23/1/1974
xi.   *The Guardian*, 25/1/1074
xii.   Letter to AR, 29/1/1974
xiii.   Interview with AR, 21/2/1998
xiv.   Letter to AR, 31/1/1998

xv.   Letter to AR, 1/2/1998
xvi.   Gwynedd Constabulary Major Incident Log (MIL), 9.00 p.m., 23/1/1974
xvii.   MIL, entries 1-4, p. 1, 23/1/1974
xviii. Colwyn Bay Police Operations Room message 8.53 p.m. 23/1/1974
xix.   MIL, entries 7, 14, p. 2/4, 23/1/1974
xx.   MIL, entries 9, 11, p. 2/3, 23/1/1974
xxi.   MIL, entry number 13, p. 3, 11.35 p.m. 23/1/1974

CHAPTER FIVE

THE NURSE'S TALE
24 January 8.30 p.m. - 10.30 p.m.

"'I remember thinking what if it's radioactive? We shouldn't really be here."

Pat Evans, 1998

The nurse, Pat Evans, and the unusual light that she and her daughters saw on the mountain slopes that night, are central to the Berwyn Mountain UFO Case. Without Pat's testimony, the event would not have achieved the degree of notoriety it has and perhaps would never have become known as a major UFO case at all.

Unfortunately, people who have never actually spoken to her about what happened, have turned Pat's personal experience into a labyrinth of claim and counter claim, freighted with their own beliefs and wishful thinking. The situation has reached the point where Pat will no longer speak to UFO researchers or - indeed - the media because she is so often misquoted or misrepresented. Yet an understanding of what Pat saw, where she saw it, and the time period in which it occurred, is fundamental to an understanding of the Berwyn case.

Pat's experience hinges on three significant points. What she saw, the location of what she saw, and what else she experienced while on the mountain road.

It is time now to recreate the event at the heart of the 'Berwyn Mountain UFO Legend' - what *really* happened to Pat Evans and what it was that she saw on the night of 23 January 1974. The following account has been compiled from primary sources and is based on Pat's words. It is what actually happened to Pat, *not* what others believe happened to her. This analysis of Pat's experience may not explain exactly what she saw, but hopefully it does something to clarify this key element of the mystery and provides a wealth of accurate evidence for future researchers to work on.

At the time of the widely felt earth rumbling and explosion, Pat was in the kitchen of her home in Llandderfel. Her two daughters were in the lounge watching TV. She recalled:

> "We'd got a Rayburn in the kitchen which was always boiling and my husband used to say one of these days it's going to explode. So when we were in the house and this huge explosion and a sort of tremor, I thought oh my god, it's happened. So I ran out into the street and had a look, could see the house was intact. By then other people were out in the village, looking and listening. I thought well, gosh, something's happened on the mountain. So I went in. My two girls were fifteen, fourteen, they were watching television in the front room. I was in the kitchen and by that time they'd come running in saying 'what was that'." [i]

Once satisfied her property was undamaged by the commotion, Pat assumed that something must have occurred on the mountains and in an attempt to find out what was happening she telephoned the local police officer. But due to the volume of telephone enquiries, the event was generating she was unable to get through and so tried another way of contacting the police.

> "I phoned Colwyn Bay HQ and, they didn't really know. They said yes, we've had reports of an explosion of sorts and we're not sure what's happened, they were very vague. I said well, could it be an aircraft, they said well it could be anything really, we don't know." [ii]

It's clear from Pat's recollections that the police switchboard operators at Colwyn Bay had no idea what had caused the explosion, and that it was Pat who suggested to them that perhaps a 'plane had come down. Being a trained and experienced nurse Pat naturally wanted to offer assistance if some kind of accident had taken place. She thought:

> "So as a nurse I'll go and see if I can help in any way if there is a disaster up there. So that was my aim you know, to go up there and see if I can help in any way if there is a disaster up there, so that was my aim you know, to go up there. I've always got bandages and things in my boot. So up I went, up to the mountain, up the mountain road." [iii]

Pat is uncertain of the precise time she left Llandderfel and what time she got to the summit of the B4391 road. However, by using a combination of her recollections, together with information she gave to the field investigators from the Institute of Geological Sciences (IGS), it is possible to be reasonably precise about the chronology of Pat's eventful evening.

In a 1998 interview, Pat told me, "I think *Steptoe and Son* was on", implying she set off sometime during the popular TV situation comedy *Steptoe and Son*. But *Steptoe and Son* was not televised on TV on 23 January 1974. However, three other situation comedies were; *The Liver Birds*, which started at 7.40 p.m. on BBC1, *Man About The House* at 8.00 p.m. on HTV, and *'Til Death Us Do Part* on BBC1 at 9.30 p.m. [iv]

As the first two comedies were televised prior to the explosion and the earth tremor it seems reasonable to suggest that Pat set off sometime during *'Til Death Us Do Part* and that in her recollections to me, twenty four years later, had confused it with Steptoe and Son which was screened later in the year.

More vital and persuasive evidence for Pat having set off during *'Til Death Us Do Part* can be found in the notes made by the IGS interviewer who spoke to Pat in the days following the event. "They tried to get the timing of it", she remembered during her interview with me, meaning the IGS had tried to establish when she left Llandderfel by asking her what was on TV at the time she left the house. The IGS notes record that Pat "Left house TV *'Till Death*. About middle, chap had just come to repair tele when went out to car". [v]

The transmission details for *'Til Death Us Do Part* was listed by the *Radio Times*, as 9.30 p.m. The episode, 'Strikes and Blackouts', featured a TV repair engineer who appears on screen exactly fifteen minutes and twenty seconds minutes into the programme. Pat's daughters were more or less ready and the car stocked with medical items, and so allowing for five minutes to leave the house, including getting in and starting the car, we can assume that Pat Evans drove away from her house at approximately 9.50 p.m. [vi]

The route she took to the B4391 mountain road was shortened by her cutting out the B4402 and using the single-track minor road that runs up side of the *Bryntirion Inn* at GR985362. This road is quite steep sided for the majority of its course, with the slopes of the hillside preventing views into the sky to the east and southeast. The timing of Pat's drive - and the significance of her use of this road - will become clear in the following chapter. After a few minutes, she turned left onto the B4391 at grid reference GR992349.

Pat remembers:

> "We kept going along the road until we reached the top of the mountain, it's quite derelict. And the girls were a bit nervous and said ooh, mum, what if someone comes out of the bushes covered in blood or whatever." [vii]

When she reached approximately grid reference GR014312, at a height of 462 metres, Pat stopped the car. Based on her leaving her house at 9.50 p.m. and with the 4.7 miles journey taking approximately ten to twelve minutes – the IGS notes record "10+ mins" -Pat would have arrived at this point at between 10.00 p.m. and 10.05 p.m.

As she and her daughters looked across the dark moorland beneath the mountains, they were astonished by what they saw.

"We could see to our left then this huge round, orange ball sitting on the mountain. And so we looked at it, couldn't make it out so we went further up to the county boundary as we called it. So we turned round and sort of parked. Now it was to the right as we were heading for home. We opened the windows and looked down and there was no sound, it was quiet, there was nothing really, just looking at this huge orange ball, and there was no windows in it, no doors and it seemed to be pulsating or glowing, like a huge ember. There were no flames shooting or anything like that, no. It was very uniform, very round in shape." Whatever it was did not appear to be obviously three dimensional, Pat remembering, "It was a flat round, looking at it like that. What it was from the sides I couldn't say." [viii]

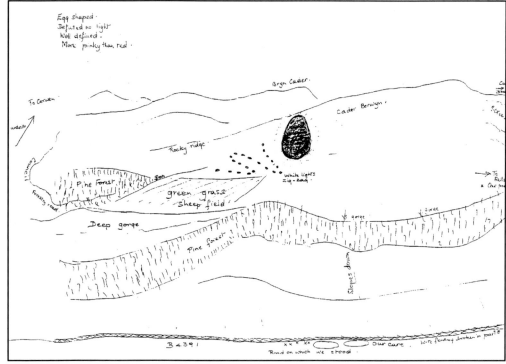

Drawing courtesy Margaret Fry

Interviewed by researchers from the IGS in 1974, just a few days after the event Pat recalled that the light was a "red blodge". The drawing the IGS made based on her description showed the light being approximately half the size of the full moon. In the same interview, she confirmed the weather conditions, remembering that "Some rain was falling – drizzle most of time." [ix]

As she watched this puzzling scene Pat noticed white lights near the light:

> "They were like torch lights, not great big torches as search-lights, more like fairy lights really from where we were standing and they seemed to be pretty uniform sort of coming toward this thing." [x]

Her 1974 IGS interview noted that she, "Could see lights above and to the right" of the lights and "Vehicle lights moving to bottom" [xi]. Pat had no idea what these lights were, but the drawing by the IGS, based on her interview looked like this:

It should be borne in mind that although Pat could see across a huge area of mountain and moorland and as far away as the Cynwyd/Corwen area, she only saw one configuration of what she assumed was torch and vehicle lights. There were no other lights of any kind visible anywhere on the mountain landscape at the time Pat Evans and her daughters were on the B4391.

Pat's observation of vehicle lights is backed up to some degree by information I was given by the son of one of Pat's friends. He remembers

> "Her telling my parents that she had seen lights of vehicles congregating in one place on the other side of the valley. This was such a remote spot and in her opinion it must have been a team of people who knew exactly what was going on, as the locals would not have been able to reach the location in such a short space of time." [xii]

As she observed the scene Pat noted, "The light changed colour to yellow and white and back again several times, but did not flicker or change shape." She and her daughters watched it for an absolute maximum of fifteen minutes before deciding that although she could not explain the object she was certain it was not a plane crash or anything similar. Mystified, she started the car up and drove home, arriving just before the TV stations closed down for the night at 10.30 p.m. [xiii]

But exactly where was the light Pat saw? This crucial point is a matter of some conjecture by UFO researchers, and the media - much of it ill informed - and the location still has not been identified with one hundred percent certainty. Based on the available evidence from Pat Evans and the two UFO researchers with whom she has entered into communication, there are two possible options, each of which present their own problems.

Before analysing these options, I would like to make it perfectly clear that I do not doubt the nature of Pat's experience. But time passes and memory fades, changes and is influenced by outside factors. The circumstances of Pat's experience and the length of time between then and her being interviewed will - undoubtedly - have unwittingly affected the accuracy of her recall. This, coupled with the fact that Pat was looking across a vast expanse of dark mountain moorland with no visual points of reference, has all helped to shroud her experience with what ifs and maybes.

FRYING TONIGHT?

Based on her interview with Pat Evans, ufologist Margaret Fry made a drawing that indicated the location of the mysterious light. This drawing, reproduced below, puts the object at - very approximately - GR042318, on a spur of Moel Sych, at the south-western end of the Berwyn range and just above Cwm yr Eithin, slightly higher than Pat Evans' vantage point on the B4391. In a 1995 letter to Margaret Fry, Pat suggests that the distance between her and the object was, "Hard to say, as the crow flies probably 2-3 miles.", which would put the light in the general area of the grid reference, above. [xiv]

However, when I interviewed Pat Evans in January 1998, her comments on the distance from the road to the light were,

> "As regards distance, I'm poor at saying how far it would be. It wasn't within walking distance see, because you have a dip like a ravine in between. Probably a mile as the crow flies, half a mile, I could take you up." [xv]

Given this confusion in recollection, the estimated distance Pat gave to me and to Margaret Fry could put the mystery light anywhere within a vast area of mountainside.

Pat very kindly drove me up on to the point on the B4391 from which her and her daughters parked and watched the object. She pointed toward where she saw it, but this indication was much further to the left than the location given to Margaret Fry. I recall Pat pointing towards a position on the hillside a few miles away and just to the right of where village streetlights are visible after dark. The photograph, reproduced opposite, I took of her pointing to the location appears to show Pat pointing in that direction. So, to where was she pointing?

When asked about the location of the light by the IGS, in January 1974, Pat said she was "Looking more or less horizontal", and the object "was slightly to right of line to Corwen lights." [xvi] By this she meant that the object was just to the right of the line of sight down to the village of Corwen, which is approximately 13.86 km (8.61 miles) miles away to the north north-east. This information was given by Pat only a few days after her experience.

In 1998, Pat told me,

> "I took a sighting, you see, knowing the area. I could see the Corwen town lights down the valley and I took a sighting with the lights." [xvii]

Whether she was seeing the Corwen or Cynwyd lights is arguable due to the lay of the land-

Nurse Pat Evans, on the B4391 in 1998, pointing toward where she saw the anomalous light- (AR)

Moel ty Uchaf circle

View across the Berwyns from the B4391

SERIAL 49 51 54 46 47.   ● Serial S1

NATURE OF INCIDENT...EXPLOSION....

GWYNEDD CONSTABULARY
MAJOR INCIDENT LOG

LOCATION:LLANDRILL

OFFICER IN CHARGE...Insp. A.R. Vaughan.

No.	Time	Date	From	To	Purport of message	Action taken	Remarks
1	2100	23/1	S157	C123	Please remain in area we are sending assistance up to you	Pc 173 – inf. marwork into 49 Ambulance HQ on stand by.	charge B ACC inf. Insp. Jones
2	2101	2.	S157	bob	Inform the Insp to contact HQ immediately.		insp in charge control room
3	2108		LT STRACHAN RAF Valley	Requesting full inf. on incident – told –	their carry out fire duty on possibly civil work in open. bring civil & military. Army are placing the RAF team at valley on STAND BY.	
4	2110	–	Pc 611 Pc 173 Insp Vaughan		arranged vehicle to scene receiving 999 calls & inf. re the incident. also receiving a primary inf. re this	See full messages

scape and the hill that rises sharply above Corwen. But she would have definitely seen the lights of Cynwyd, situated on the B4401 toward Llandrillo. If Pat was accurate in her reference to the Cynwyd (or indeed Corwen) street lights then it is highly unlikely the light was situated at the point she indicated to Margaret Fry, as this was more or less directly east of Pat's parked car.

A SITE FOR SORE EYES

During the course of their interviews with the IGS, each person and each relevant point on the landscape was given an individual reference number. Pat Evans was C78 and her location marked on the map as C100. We do not know where exactly Pat told the IGS interviewer the light was, but on the IGS master map a very faint line has been drawn from point C100 to point C64, approximately 4.99 km (3.10 miles) away. This area of land is just to the right of a direct line of sight from Cynwyd and would have appeared as such in relation to the street-lights at night. It is logical to assume that either Pat told the IGS investigator the light was seen at that location, or that they deduced it from what she told them. [xviii] The significance of point C64, the area around it and what took place there will become apparent in the next chapter.

One significant point to consider is that if Pat saw the light high on the side of Moel Sych, as the Margaret Fry drawing indicates, it would have been clearly visible to Pat for at least two kilometres prior to where she first records noticing it. If the light had been in this location then Pat and her daughters would have been travelling towards it. Conversely, if the light had been near point C64 on the IGS map, she would have been unlikely to notice it until the point she stopped on the B4391 just past Pont Cwm Pydew, where the forest ends.

To confuse matters further, I contacted Pat in April 2010, sending her a map and a copy of the Margaret Fry drawing, with both of the possible locations for the light marked up. I asked her to indicate where she believed the light had been on January 23 1974. Pat clearly indicated that the light was in the area described to Margaret Fry in 1995 and emphatically not at GR043352 (Point C64 on the IGS map) [xix]. So, despite Pat believing she is certain where the mysterious light was, her accounts are contradictory and the puzzle of exactly where the light was located remains as yet unsolved.

BLINDED BY THE LIGHT

And just what was the light that Pat and her daughters saw? At the time of writing, this too remains a mystery. We know from Pat's descriptions of the light that it was 'bright red, like coal fire red' (1974), 'Changed colour to yellow and white and back again [to red]' (1974), 'Red' (1996), and 'Orange' (1998).

Pat maintains the light wasn't projecting light in a beam or burning like a fire but, 'Glowing... pulsating' (1996), 'Pulsating or glowing, like a huge ember' (1998), 'Shimmering/ pulsating' (2010).

And the light had clear definition, 'Perfect circle' (1974), 'Round... spherical' (1996), 'Very round... a flat round... what it was from the sides I couldn't say' (1998), 'Round' (2010). Size wise, she has described the light as, 'Large' [drawn as half the size of the full moon] (1974), 'Huge' (1996), 'Huge' (1998).

Pat's description of the colour, definition and size of the mysterious light has remained largely consistent over the years. The light seemed to be much larger than either the torch or the vehicle lights that were approaching or adjacent to it. If the IGS drawing depicting the light as being half the size of the full moon is correct then it would have been enormous and visible for miles around, not just to Pat, her daughters and whoever was in the group with the vehicle and torches.

Once again, we are dealing with the vagaries of human perception. Without impugning Pat's integrity in any way I would suggest that several factors were at work, making the light appear larger than it was. At the time, Pat was acting on the belief that she may be attending the site of an aircraft disaster and therefore may have been expecting to see a large source of light indicating a downed 'plane. In addition, she was on an unlit road in the depths of winter. The night was pitch-black with no moon or stars. A light drizzle was falling. Pat was looking out across a huge area of dark and featureless landscape with no points of reference other than what she believed was vehicle and torch lights. Under such conditions, it would be entirely feasible that she perceived the light as being much bigger than it actually was. Nonetheless, we must accept that whatever Pat and her daughters were observing was a bright, self-contained light that appeared much bigger than torch or vehicle lights.

HALT! WHO GOES THERE?

Several versions of the Berwyn myth claim that on her return journey to Llandderfel on the B4391, Pat was stopped and ordered off the mountain by police and military personnel. This did not happen, but the idea that she was stopped has become firmly embedded in the Berwyn myth, bolstering the idea that the authorities were aware that a UFO had come down and were securing the area. How this canard entered the myth is both intriguing and instructive and tells us a great deal about how easily unfounded rumours can spread about a UFO case and is worth briefly exploring.

Pat Evans' experience was not brought into the public domain until the mid 1990s, when ufologist Margaret Fry, recently retired to north Wales, began to gather anecdotes about the case from locals. Unfortunately, she did not carry out taped interviews and only kept brief notes. Fry allegedly told UFO author Jenny Randles that Pat Evans had claimed she had been stopped by the military and/or police. As a result, in part of her book about UFO crashes, *UFO Retrievals*, Jenny wrote:

> "Police and military forces, who had been even closer to the object, passed her on the way down the mountain. She explained why she was there and asked what was happening. Nobody answered her questions, except to say she would have to leave; no one unauthorised was al-

lowed up there. So they escorted her down to the main road. Because she was afraid for her daughters' safety, she did not argue and left." [xx]

This bombshell was avidly picked up on by several other writers who repeated it in various books and magazines, and within a short space of time it became accepted as a 'fact' that Pat Evans had been escorted from the mountain road by the authorities. The implication being, of course, that the military were aware of what Pat Evans had seen and didn't want civilians going near it. If it could be proven that Pat was stopped and moved on by the military it would be a major boost to those theorists who believe a physical craft, perhaps even an extraterrestrial craft, was what the nurse saw.

But as with much about the Berwyn case, it's just not that simple.

The first obstacle to such claims is that there is no official documentation to suggest it happened. Whereas there is a comprehensive official paper trail for every other element of the case and Police, MOD and RAF records exist detailing most aspects of what took place on the night of 23 January 1974. Of course, conspiracy theorists will contest that this is because all trace of a military or police presence has been covered up. But it would be reasonable to suggest that the Police Incident Log for the night would at least allude tangentially to police officers being sent on the B4391 or that one of the police officers interviewed since 1974 would have spoken out. Yet there is no hint in any documentation, official or otherwise, of this happening.

This lack of official evidence brings us back to the only person who really knows what took place, Pat Evans herself. During my 1998 interview with Pat, I asked her if she had seen anyone else, to which she replied, "Not a living soul...I didn't see a soldier or a policeman, I saw no-one." [xxi]

The following morning Pat was due on shift at a Wrexham hospital. She left Llandderfel just after 6 a.m. and saw no sign of any military or police activity in the area. Pat Evans has always been puzzled both by the events of 24 January 1974 and what she and her daughters saw. When I asked her what she thought it was she answered, "People didn't really talk. It was a laugh for a short space of time, I didn't lose any sleep." [xxii]

Just what this 'mystery' was may be either illuminated or perpetuated in the next chapter as we examine what two other groups of people were doing during the same time frame Pat Evans was on the B4391.

NOTES

i.   Interview with AR 31/1/98
ii.   Interview with AR 31/1/98

iv.   Interview with AR 31/1/98. Radio Times, January 1974
v.   IGS notes C78, January 1974
vi.   Steptoe and Son, Strikes and Blackouts, transmitted 23/1/74
vii.   Interview with AR 31/1/98
viii.   Interview with AR 31/1/98
ix.   IGS notes, C78, January 1974
x.   Interview with AR 31/1/98
xi.   IGS notes, C78, January 1974
xii.   Letter from A. Roberts, Bala, 3/2/98
xiii.   Interview with AR 31/1/98
xiv.   Letter to Margaret Fry, 23/10/95
xv.   Interview with AR 31/1/98
xvi.   IGS notes, C78, January 1974
xv.   Interview with AR 31/1/98
xvi.   IGS notes, C78, January 1974
xvii   Letter and map from Pat Evans, 12/4/10
xviii   *UFO Retrievals*, Jenny Randles, Blandford 1995, p 112-121
xix   Interview with AR 31/1/98
xx   Interview with AR 31/1/98

CHAPTER SIX

AN INSPECTOR CALLS

23 January 1974
8.30 p.m. - 11.30 p.m.

"I want to commandeer your Landrover"

Inspector Glyn Evans

At the same time Pat Evans was being baffled on the B4391, three other groups of people were becoming enmeshed in the Berwyn mystery. As Pat drove onto the mountain road that night in January 1974, the destinies of several police officers, a farmer's son and his neighbour, and a group of poachers unwittingly became entwined with hers.

AN ARRESTING SIGHT

At exactly 9.05 p.m., Inspector Vaughan at Colwyn Bay Police HQ alerted Inspector Glyn Evans at Dolgellau Police Station, to the likelihood of a major incident having taken place in the Llandrillo area. The information Inspector Evans was given led him to believe an aircraft disaster had occurred. He left Dolgellau immediately by car and drove at speed to Bala Police Station where he met Police Sergeant Elfred Roberts. A brief chat took place before they set off for Llandrillo in the Bala Police van. Sgt Roberts took the wheel and as they drove quickly through the night they speculated as to what might have taken happened to generate the massive volume of 999 calls to the various police stations. [i]

About a mile from Llandrillo, at just after 9.35 p.m. they witnessed an unusual phenomenon. At GR014370 Inspector Evans saw a "green flare" which was travelling to the east in an arched trajectory. This sighting lasted no more than five seconds. Sgt Roberts also saw the light and described it as a "green arching light with sort of blue tinges to the edges". [ii]

According to Inspector Evans' report, they arrived in Llandrillo at about 9.40 p.m. to find the streets thronged with villagers puzzled as to what was happening and wanting to relate their experiences to the police. Curiously, no one in the village appears to have seen the green 'flare' seen by the police officers. This was the second, possibly third such 'flare' to have been seen during the evening so far.

Evans and Roberts had a brief conversation with Sgt Owen, the Llandrillo police officer. Sgt Owen brought the two officers up to speed with what the villagers had experienced over the last eighty minutes. The Inspector and Sergeant left Sgt Owen in Llandrillo and headed for the area of mountains where people indicated they had seen lights and where the noise appeared to have come from. A problem immediately arose. The officers were in a standard police van unsuited to off road driving and neither of them was familiar with the landscape. A vehicle and someone to guide them over the featureless terrain of the Berwyns was required. As they drove up Berwyn Street, the dead end road leading from the centre of Llandrillo to the mountainside, they decided to stop at a farm en route to seek assistance.

BOMBS AWAY?

On the evening of 23 January fourteen-year-old farmer's son Huw Lloyd was settling down to an evening in front of the TV at Garthian, his family farm (GR 365032). His parents were out for the evening and Huw was at home with his two sisters. Also present was Enoch, an older neighbour who had called round to watch an episode of *The World at War* which featured the Thousand Bomber Raid.

Just after 8.30 p.m., they all heard and felt the earth tremor, causing ornaments and furniture in the house to rattle and the lights to dim. Rushing into the farmyard, they looked round and checked on the livestock but could see nothing that could have caused the disturbance. So, mystified, they went back inside. Within seconds, the phone began to ring as neighbours called to see if anyone else had heard the noise and felt the tremor. No-one they spoke to had any explanation so they returned indoors and settled down to watch TV again. Huw estimates that it was between twenty and thirty minutes later that there was a knock at the farmhouse door. He answered it to find at least five police officers in the farmyard including an Inspector. Based on the times given in official police records this must have been at about 9.45 p.m., although Huw's more vague timing puts it earlier, at around 9.20 p.m. [iii]

"We want your Landrover; we want you to go up to the Berwyn. We believe it's a 'plane crash", the Inspector said, and asked Huw if he would drive them up there. Huw did not recognise any of the officers and believed they were not local. Enoch asked one of them where they were from, and received the reply "Barmouth". This answer caused a great deal of speculation and confusion. If any of the police officers had travelled from Barmouth it would have been virtually impossible for them to reached Llandrillo in the 40-50 minutes that had elapsed since the rumblings. [iv]

The distance from Barmouth to Llandrillo is 35 miles, along winding roads. Huw commented, "It takes an hour to come from Barmouth you know, a bit of a mystery. Looking back, why did they turn up so quickly?" This has led to conjecture by conspiracy theorists that the police from Barmouth already knew what was going on and had travelled to the area before the earth tremor at 8.38 p.m. In fact, as we now know from the police documents cited at the start of this chapter, the Inspector and Sergeant had not come from Barmouth at all, but from Dolgellau and Bala, both within easy driving distance of Llandrillo.

Huw checked that the Landrover had enough fuel and the police officers climbed in through the rear doors. Being only fourteen, Huw asked Enoch to drive the Landrover up the road leading to the forest track, and so they set off. After less than half a mile, where the tarmac road ended and the rough, stony forest track began, they had to stop. An abandoned car was blocking the track. A couple of the police officers got out and after some struggle managed to move the car out of the way. The vehicle was unlocked so they removed the tax disc, an old police trick to ensure the owners would have to come forward to reclaim it and thus reveal their identity. [v]

As an illustration of the problems that occur with peoples' recollections of events after the passage of a number of years, neither Inspector Evans nor Sgt Roberts cannot recall them stopping to move the car out of the way. The Berwyn case is littered with a number of these odd occurrences but it is necessary to accept that witness perception and memory is fallible and changes with the passage of time. Whether or not Evans or Roberts could remember stopping to move the poachers' car we know from Huw Lloyd and the poachers themselves that it was moved.

RUN RABBIT RUN!

The car may have been deserted but its occupants were nearby, hidden out of sight on the other side of a nearby wall. This was no courting couple, but a team of poachers coming down off the mountains after an evening of hunting. Interviewed a few days after the event by the IGS, one of the poachers said he was part of a team of four who were out 'lamping'. Lamping is a method of hunting involving a bright lamp that is shone onto prey such as rabbits. The rabbit will become motionless in the beam, allowing it to be shot. If secrecy is necessary, a hunting dog is sent to run silently and unseen down the outside of the beam to snatch the animal. In this case, the poachers told the IGS they were using a lamp constructed from a car spot lamp attached to a car battery fitted with a halogen bulb. Such a light would have projected a very bright pencil beam of light, which could have been seen from several miles away if shone vertically.

The poachers had parked their car at about 8.00 p.m. and walked the short distance to the place they planned to shoot, in the area of GR 354043 (Point 64 on the IGS map). They had not been hunting long when three out of the four heard a slight rumble, which they discounted as being of any significance. Rabbit was their intended prey but Snipe were also present on the mountainside that night. This bird when disturbed flies up and almost hovers before flying off. One of the poachers told the research team from Firefly TV they were pointing their powerful lamp beam up at the Snipe as they rose as well as casting their beam around for rabbit. [vi]

The poachers were hunting in exactly the same area as the 'beams' of light which had been seen on the mountainside by Llandrillo villagers after the earth tremor. The poachers did not see beams of light other than their own. Thus, we can be certain that the poachers caused the beams of light seen in Llandrillo for up to fifteen minutes after the earth tremor. Intriguingly, although they were on open mountainside at the time of the earth tremor the poachers did not see any of the 'glows' or flashes' of light as reported from Llandrillo. Nor, indeed, did they report seeing the earlier meteorite. Whether this is yet another unsolved mystery or whether the poacher's were just looking the other way at the time, we will never know.

As they returned to their car, the poachers heard vehicles coming up the track toward them and they recognised Huw, and could see the peaked cap of the Inspector in the Landrover. Not knowing what was happening and half out of instinct they jumped behind a wall, continuing on their way when the Landrovers (one of the poachers believes that there was more than one vehicle) had passed. Just before reaching the car the poachers met a group of local police officers who said, "There's an aircraft come down boys, did you see anything?". [vii]

BLINDED BY THE LIGHT

Enoch continued to drive the Landrover until they reached the mountain gate at GR 044354, where he asked Huw to take over. They stopped the vehicle. The night was completely silent except for the gentle hiss of the falling drizzle the occasional bleating of sheep. The Inspector asked Huw if he would take the Landrover through the gate, out on to the open mountainside, which he did, and they travelled slowly onwards, some police officers with torches walking alongside the vehicle. Sgt Roberts remembers:

> "When we were on top of the mountain we actually used our own torches to look round to see if we could see any crater or seat of fire or something that would be some sort of explanation." [viii]

Suddenly, the entire mountain lit up with brilliant white light. The light came from the south east, behind the brow of the hill, in the general direction of Llangynog, appearing to emanate from the ground. Huw estimated it could have lasted for five or six seconds at most, during which time the pitch-black mountainside was illuminated enough for the police officers' uniforms and faces to be clearly visible.

> "Next thing, the whole place just ... lit up", remembered Huw Lloyd in 1998. He described the light as being as bright as halogen head-lights on a car. [ix]

Because they were half expecting to find a disaster on the mountains, the police officers' first thoughts were that they had seen a distress flare from a crashed aircraft and wanted to get back in the vehicle and drive toward it. They asked Huw if he could do this but he explained he could not drive to where the light appeared to come from because of the rough terrain. Huw though they could go some way toward it, so the party drove off again. It is uncertain exactly how far the police went, but the IGS master map places them at in the area around GR 057352

...ry .... 1ed .... ate/time
.... Nto @ .... Tne
.... Tne
....Tme
....hrs
....te/Tne
....oity by
Type of Search ....
.... Nno.
Weather Conditions 10
....Party .... 3 ...1
No of Casualties............. Tot.. 1
Stretcher......... .... SNC 1
Dead ....
Vehicle Mileage
3 ton x 2 .... .le Involved .....
LWB Amb ....tion/Station°..... ate/time
LWB KFT .... Int.... ...... ate/time
SWB .... (........ words not applicable)
Comments on Equipment ..../A
....
Narrative.- ....
....
redused ....

Extract from RAF Valley Mountain Rescue Team Log

AERIAL PHENOMENA ENQUIRY NETWORK

COPY OF INITIAL REPORT

CONCERNING NORTH WALES ... BRITISH AUTHORITY.

... 24.JAN ...

S.N.O.
PRIORY:
VIA W/T LINK 04.
PRIORITY ONE.

... REFERENCE CENTRE.
... AGENTS 71 & 347.
Case No. 174L.74-71/...
LOCALITY:- ... NORTH WALES.
INCIDENT:- LANDING AND CONTACT (ALMOST PROVEN)
RECOMMENDED ACTION:- ...
DURATION:- ...
... OUT:- ...
WERE EQUIP:- ...

... (... 25.JAN.74).
NUMBER OF EXTRA PERSONNEL EMPLOYED:- 4 (RECOMMEND AT PHASE ONE TO BE ...
ANY OTHER COMMENTS:- Request two sets of Initial Report forms to my
address and that of ...

... having interviewed ... as instructed,

found him to be very ... He was ...

... occupied and his description of the craft and others I was more

... that ... to ... have been ... though this

... he is an ex-soldier ... Captain "Adams"

Scout Ship with a few ... and ... at

... of ...

... described ... to the Lake District

... and ...

... to

A...R.N. 1974.

One of the APEN documents

(Point R14), a sloping area below Cader Bronwen, the main feature of which is a large bog that would have hindered further progress.

Huw Thomas and the police were not the only people to witness this bright flash of light. It is precisely *because* there were so many other witnesses we can be certain what time it occurred and what it was. Official records provide times and prove the light was not purely local to the Berwyn Mountains area. The Ministry of Defence (MoD) received a report from Chigwell Row in Essex of something the "Size of the Moon, green in colour, with a long tail", travelling east to west just before 10.00 p.m. Another witness, from Mill Hill in north London was looking in a north westerly direction saw a, "White vertical track in the sky – green flash occurred before it disappeared over the horizon". This too was witnessed just before 10.00 p.m.[x]

Several people in Llandrillo reported seeing a bright white/green light at times varying from 9.45 p.m. to 10.10 p.m. At just after 9.45 p.m. one witness saw a 'flare' that was, "Yellow to orange but as bits fell low some deep green seen in it." Another saw a "Blue greenish flare...very long from head to tail and transient." The light was last logged, by the Holyhead Coastguard station on the Isle of Anglesey at just after 10.00 p.m., "I logged sighting a very bright meteorite or shooting star in the sky heading due east." The times given by the villagers may be vague but those given by the MoD and the Holyhead Coastguard are exact and reflect sightings of a very bright bolide meteor, the last one of several seen throughout the evening.[xi]

The MoD file contains details of an investigation which was carried out on the behalf of the British Astronomical Society by Dr Hindley, formerly of Leeds University, who told them, "At 9.59 p.m. a fireball was visible over most of the United Kingdom. It was estimated that the fireball descended from about 120 kilometres to a height of about 35 kilometres before disintegrating... Reports of sightings of the fireball were received from various parts of the UK, including Somerset, Norfolk, Manchester and Edinburgh."[xii]

Curiously, Nurse Pat Evans and her daughters did not refer to having seen this bright meteor. Considering how bright it was, and from how far afield it was viewed, this appears - initially at least - to be a mystery. The most likely explanation for Pat not seeing the meteor, based on the time of them leaving their house in Llandderfel, is that at the time of the bolide passing overhead they had just turn up the steep and enclosed road by the Bryntirion Inn and were not in a position to see it.

A TANGLE OF PARADOX AND CONUNDRUM

How do the activities of the poachers and the presence of the police and Huw Lloyd on the mountainside have any bearing on Pat Evans and what she saw? Well, there is a clear line of sight from where Nurse Pat Evans was parked on the B4391 to the entire area stretching from the mountain gate to point R14 and a wide area around it. The distance between Pat Evans' location and that of the police and Huw Lloyd is approximately 3.20 miles (5.16 km).

In my original investigation of the Berwyn Mountain UFO case, I found a reference in the IGS files to the poachers having met Huw Lloyd and the police on the mountain. As the poachers were known to be carrying a powerful lamp, I speculated that perhaps this is what Pat had seen, the beam of the lamp being distorted in the drizzle and appearing much larger than it was. All the times fitted and a poacher's lamp, misperceived in mist and drizzle by someone expecting to see evidence of a crashed aircraft appeared to solve the mystery. [xiii]

However, new information from the poachers, obtained in 2008 by the Firefly TV researchers completely confounded this theory. As a result, the light seen by Pat Evans and the identity of those responsible for the vehicle and torchlights seen near it were once again thrown into mystery.[xiv]

Yet despite this misperception on my part, very close attention should be paid to the time frame under discussion in this chapter, the locations of all parties and to just what they were doing. The times of each of the three parties are exact to within a few minutes, their locations known to within a few yards. With such detailed knowledge, the puzzle of the light Pat saw should be easily resolvable. Yet it is not. Something about the Pat Evans/Police/Poacher/ Farmer's son scenario does not quite add up. The conundrum can be broken down into the following elements:

- We know that Pat Evans and her daughters drove and parked on the B4391 between approximately 10.00 p.m. and 10.15 p.m., looking at a large ball of light that had at least one vehicle and several torch lights adjacent to it.
- We know that Huw Lloyd, his neighbour and at least five police officers in one, or possibly two, Landrovers were on an area of the mountainside that was clearly visible from Pat Evans' vantage point. We also know they were there between just before 10.00 p.m. until about 10.15 p.m., based on the police timings and their sighting of the bright bolide meteor at 10.00 p.m.
- In all of her interviews, beginning with the one she gave the IGS in 1974 Pat only ever recalls seeing one set of vehicles and torches, and no other lights on the mountains. There was no obstruction to her line of sight as the weather conditions, while wet and windy, were clear enough for her to see the streetlights in Cynwyd and or Corwen, 11 km distant (6.83 miles).

Based on these factors, logic suggests that either:

- There were two lots of vehicles out on the mountainside with people walking alongside them with torches at exactly the same time and less than 2.5 (3.75 km) miles apart, one group of which was the police and Huw Lloyd.

Or

- The vehicles and torches Pat Evans was looking at were those of the police and Huw Lloyd. Both these possibilities have their problems:

- If the first option is true, then who were the other people? Why did Huw and the police not see their lights or hear their vehicles? Why did no one in Llandrillo come forward to say it was they or that they had seen vehicles going up or coming down the track to this area of land? Considering the local and national media publicity the Berwyn Mountain UFO case has generated it seems inconceivable that if they were locals their identity would have remained hidden for over 36 years.

- If the second option is true, then the huge light that was seen by Pat Evans, based on her testimony and the drawing in the IGS field notes, was in between or very near the vehicle driven by Huw Lloyd and the police officers searching the mountainside with their torches. Yet none of that party saw anything at all other than the bolide meteor at 10.00 p.m.

This conundrum lies at the heart of the Berwyn Mountain UFO case. Every other element of the case can explained rationally using official documents which can be cross-referenced with witness statements. However, what Pat Evans saw, where it was and who was closing in on it remains as a gigantic question mark hanging over the Berwyn Mountain UFO case. As long as this question remains unresolved claims of a crashed or landed UFO, dead aliens, a military crash retrieval team and a government cover up will continue.

COMING DOWN AGAIN

After some time spent fruitlessly searching the mountainside Huw and the police drove back down the forest track and onto the tarmac road. There they met several other police officers, on foot and in cars. There was much speculation about what might have happened but no one had anything relevant to say so Huw returned to his farm and to bed. The police dispersed shortly afterwards.

At 11.30 p.m. that night, the MIL recorded, "All the men are down off the mountain- nothing found but they did see a green flare in the direction of Llangynog." By now, the police were convinced there was no possibility of an aircraft having crashed on the mountains and calls were made to Merioneth Fire Service standing them down. Another entry in the MIL noted, "Token search will be undertaken in the morning." [xv]

The following morning, and indeed the next few days would see a great deal of civilian and official activity in and around Llandrillo and the northern slopes of the Berwyn Mountains that would contribute to the rumours of a cover up. Whether these rumours were based on fact or fiction will be discussed in the next chapter.

NOTES

i.   Letter from G. Evans to IGS, 30/1/74
ii.   Letter from G. Evans to IGS, 30/1/74
iii. Interview with AR 31/1/98

iv.   Interview with AR 31/1/98
v.   Interview with AR 31/1/98
vi.   Firefly Film and Television Productions, interview with Iyan Roberts, 2008
vii.   Firefly Film and Television Productions, interview with Iyan Roberts, 2008
viii. Firefly Film and Television Productions, interview with Elfred Roberts, 2008
ix.   Interview with AR 31/1/98
x.   AIR/2/19083, 14/2/74, Letter to Mr S. Dee
xi.   Holyhead Coastguard Log, 23/1/74
xii.   AIR/2/19083, 14/2/74, file note to Mr Crowther, 9/5/74
xiii. *Fire on the Mountain*, The UFOs That Never Were, Randles J, Clarke, D, Roberts A, London House, 1980
xiv.   Firefly Film and Television Productions, interview with Iyan Roberts, 2008
xvi.   MIL entry, p.3, 23/1/1974

CHAPTER SEVEN

THE MORNING AFTER THE NIGHT BEFORE
24/1/74 – 31/1/74

"It could be as big as a house to have the kind of effect this thing has caused"
Dr. David Matthews

Midnight saw Wednesday 23rd January slipping silently into Thursday the 24th. The villages of Llandrillo and Llandderfel were quiet silent; Pat Evans was sleeping soundly and the police and farmer's search party were long since down from the mountain slopes. There were no further sightings of balls of fire in the sky or of mysterious beams and lights on the hills. The only activity of note was at 0.10 a.m. when the RAF Valley Mountain Rescue Team arrived in Llandrillo. They immediately bedded down for the night in preparation for a search that would start at dawn.

News of the previous night's events was spreading rapidly and had already reached the media. The Radio 2 news headline at midnight was 'A Mysterious Explosion in North Wales'.

What took place in the days following the 23rd is crucial. The Berwyn mountain UFO legend claims that a UFO had either crashed or landed and that military and police teams had searched for and removed this craft to Porton Down. There is no evidence of such a retrieval team being present during the evening of the 23rd. The legend also claims that there was a large military presence in days following the event and also that areas of the mountains were cordoned off and farmers prevented from tending their stock. If evidence were found to substantiate a military presence in and around Llandrillo in the immediate aftermath of the 23rd, it would go some way to bolster the claims of those who believe a UFO was involved.

In the days following the 23rd, Inspector Evans and Sgt Roberts discussed the possibility there could have been a military operation to which they were not privy, because the various lights seen throughout the evening had puzzled them. But, based on what they knew and on their lengthy experience as police officers they discounted this theory. Neither of them had any evidence of a military presence and nor had any of their police officers. It would have been impossible for a military operation to take place without senior police officers such as Inspector Owen being aware of it.

A FRUITLESS SEARCH?

I am going to examine in detail what took place in the days and weeks following the event, pieced together from the recollections of those who lived, worked and visited the Llandrillo area, media reports and official documents. Drawing on this complex web of source material it should become apparent if there is any evidence of unusual police and military activity in the area and if so what the nature and purpose of that activity was.

The Mountain Rescue Team from RAF Valley was awake and on the move at first light on Thursday morning. Huw Lloyd saw them drive past his farm and up toward the mountain gate where they started a search lasting several hours. Mona Scholz, from Corwen, was also up early, taking children to bus stops to catch the school bus. Her account is the earliest civilian account we have from the 24th, and makes for interesting reading, "As I was going through Llandrillo, at about twenty past seven, there were these soldiers." The soldiers stopped Mona and queried her destination before allowing her to continue. But this was no sinister UFO crash retrieval team, "At a guess I would say they were territorials. I think there were probably a couple of local lads in it." Mona believed the soldiers were from a Territorial Army unit based in Wrexham. Some of them were walking across the fields in the direction of Cader Bronwen accompanied by the Sgt Owen, local police officer. [i]

Rhiannon Evans was living on a farm in Llandrillo and recalls the events of 24th January clearly. The following day she saw "...quite a lot of Lorries and things like that going up there", and believes they were Army vehicles. No one else saw any Army vehicles, so what Rhiannon saw is debatable, but the most likely candidates are probably the RAF Valley Mountain Rescue Landrovers. [ii]

Huw Lloyd, the farmer's son who, on the previous evening had driven the police onto the slopes of Cader Bronwen had taken the day off school. He remembers a great deal of activity including, "A lot of policemen again, and a neighbour, took a load of policemen up with a tractor." Besides the mountain rescue team, he also saw a few helicopters flying over the mountains. Later in the morning two people in a large safari Landrover arrived in his farmyard, requesting to be guided onto the slopes. [iii] This was Dr Ron Maddison from Keele University in Staffordshire, who arrived with Dr Aneurin Evans, a colleague from the physics department.

Dr. Maddison first heard about the Berwyn events on Radio 4 during the previous evening. Although the news report speculated that an aircraft might have crashed, Ron believed the description sounded like a meteorite. On arrival in Llandrillo, Maddison spoke to Sgt Owen who directed them to Huw Lloyd's farm.

As he had done with the police on the previous evening, Huw guided the pair onto the high mountains but they found nothing of significance. Far below, they could see the mountain rescue people searching the area to which Huw had taken the police on the night before. Ron is adamant there was no military presence in Llandrillo or on the mountains that day and that "At no time was the area cordoned-off by anyone!"[iv]

Although media sources were reporting that the rumbling and explosion at 8.38 p.m. on the 23rd was an earth tremor this was not widely known to people of Llandrillo and surrounding areas. This part of the mystery at least was soon to be at least partially resolved.

At 9.10 a.m., the police contacted the Seismological department at Edinburgh University to ask if the seismographs had recorded anything that indicated an earth tremor in the Llandrillo area on the previous evening. The response was negative but hopeful:

> "However, with the trigonometrical distances involved we will be unable to locate its location but we should be able to say if it is an earth tremor or an impact tremor."

In other words when they had carried out further calculations they would know whether it had been a meteor or an earth tremor.[v]

The entries in Gwynedd Constabulary's Major Incident Log continued overnight into the 24th January. At 10.12 a.m., the MIL noted a phone call from Corporal Booth of the Army Bomb Disposal Unit based in Hereford. Booth requested they call him when the location of the "explosion" was discovered so he could travel to Llandrillo to "investigate". No further information exists regarding this query but it seems odd that if a military cover up were in place other military units would be allowed to call the police to offer their services.[vi]

At 10.50 a.m., the Seismological department in Edinburgh 'phoned the police back to inform them, "The seismological readings indicate a tremor of magnitude 4 which is of earthquake proportions. We are unable to state if it is of impact origin or a natural earth tremor." This ambiguity notwithstanding, and as the search parties had failed to find any trace of a meteor impact on the Berwyn Mountains, it was clear that the rumblings and explosion that took place at 8.38 were caused by an earthquake and nothing else. Over this entry in the MIL, in different handwriting, someone had written "RESULT". [vii]

Following this nugget of information, at 12.30 p.m., the MIL records that Inspector Evans made the decision to call off the police search and all officers ordered back to their respective police stations. The police interpretation of the seismologists' information was that nothing had impacted crashed or landed on the Berwyn Mountains. And with that, the involvement of the police ended, officially at least. This still left the mysterious lights, glows, beams and the unusual light witnessed by Pat Evans, but these were of no interest to the police force.

The RAF Valley Mountain Rescue Team had stood down at 11.50 a.m., just prior to the police search being called off. The MIL recorded that the VRMTs tentative conclusions of the "Strong possibility that having regard to the fact that no aircraft has been reported missing that the occurrence was caused by a natural phenomenon such as a very large meteorite. No further search will be carried out." [viii]

When Sgt Oldham submitted his report on the search there was little narrative to illuminate the above statement. His report noted, "VMRT requested to investigate lights and noise on hillside. Advance party covered relevant area with negative results. Incident produced much local excitement."

DO THEY MEAN US?

The events were featured extensively on the radio and TV news throughout the 24th and even a few newspapers were quick enough off the mark and gave it some coverage. *The Times* ran a short piece headed Explosion starts Meteorite Hunt in Wales, while *The Daily Telegraph* went with Explosion Heard from Mountain. *The Daily Mirror* gave it the most column inches with What Went Bang in the Night? Each paper reported the noises and earth movements at 8.38 p.m., the lights seen on the mountainside and the police search, speculating that a meteor or an earth tremor was the cause. Vaughn Biscoe was quoted as saying:

> "It sounded like an earthquake. Our cottage shook so much that my wife and I thought it was going to topple over. We saw a light up the mountain."

The Shropshire Star discounted the meteorite theory after interviewing Flight Sgt Oldham of the RAF Valley Mountain Rescue Team. "A meteorite, even a large one, would be unlikely to cause a tremor that far away" Odiham commented. [ix]

A spokesperson for the Coastguard Service was widely quoted. He said that several stations had been inundated with claims of "green flares".

> "We are pretty certain it was a meteorite shower. We ourselves witnessed the end of one of them in a white flash which was too bright to have been lightning." The press also reported that ships in the Irish Sea had also reported the bright lights. [x]

Later in the day Ron Maddison flew over the Berwyn Mountains in a helicopter provided by the Manchester based Granada Television, who based a news item that evening on his flight. Although the helicopter criss-crossed the area for an hour Ron could see no signs of a crater or other unusual ground markings. Ron also used his contacts to persuade RAF Valley on Anglesey to overfly the area and take photographs from a reconnaissance aircraft. He later studied the many photographs taken and commented, "The resolution was certainly high enough to be able to detect fresh disturbances – none were found." [xi]

X MARKS THE SPOT

LLANDRILLO
Chester
LLANDDERFEL
WALES

Aliens crash riddle would baffle Scully and Mulder

EXCLUSIVE

BAFFLED Government chiefs have been sitting on a real-life X-File that would send TV sleuths Scully and Mulder into orbit.

Alien corpses were secretly recovered from a Welsh mountainside in the Seventies and transported to the country's most secret defence base, say UFO investigators.

The claims by a retired serviceman have been revealed on the eve of a new series of Britain's favourite sci-fi programme.

Shocked

Dead aliens were found on the slopes of the Berwyn mountain range and then transported to the hush-hush weapons research establishment at Porton Down, Wilts. In his statement, the serviceman told how his unit responded to a major alert in January 1974.

He said he was present when bodies of aliens were loaded on to an Army transporter after a flying saucer crash.

The incident allegedly happened near the remote communities of Llandderfel and Llandrillo after locals reported a ball of light streaking across the skies and falling to Earth with "an enormous bang".

The Army officer said he and four other soldiers were sent to

■■ IAN BRANDES

the scene and ordered to load two boxes on to their vehicles then drive to Porton Down.

He claimed: "The boxes were opened by staff at the facility in our presence. We were shocked to see two creatures, which had been placed inside decontamination suits.

"When the suits were fully opened, it was obvious that the creatures were not of this world. The bodies were about five to six feet tall, humanoid in shape, but so thin they looked almost skeletal with covered skin."

The witness claims to have met other servicemen with even more sensational information.

They told him they had also transported aliens to Porton Down — but their cargo was still **ALIVE.**

A spokesman for UFO magazine said he was certain that the retired officer was genuine.

Despite the time lapse of 22 years, there seems to be increas-

ing evidence that something mysterious happened in the Berwyn mountain range in late January 1974.

Armed

In a separate investigation, top UFO expert Jenny Randles also claims a flying saucer crashed in the area.

She says a local nurse saw armed soldiers guarding the wreckage of the space craft.

But the Defence Ministry has "no knowledge" of the incident.

1996 Daily Star clipping, showing how the case had become legendary

... London board of inquiry yesterday was said to be the direct cause of a rail crash in which ten people died.

The twisted blue plate 3ft. by 2ft. was the remains of the battery box lid of diesel locomotive 1007, the Western Talisman.

As the engine pulled 11 coaches towards Oxford at 70 m.p.h. on December 19 last year, the lid came open, hit the platform at Ealing Broadway station and then smashed into the mechanism controlling a set of points at Longfield Junction near West Ealing station, the inquiry heard.

The impact changed the points and the entire train, carrying 650 passengers, swung from the fast track to a relief line and was derailed.

As well as the ten killed 53 people were taken to hospital.

'I think you will agree with me that the story of accident happened is sive one,' said Lieut Ian McNaughton, cha the accident.

'There is no doubt one's mind what we ing about.'

The battery box li was ripped from tive by the impact,

Hunt for thing that went bump in the night

Daily Mail Reporter

SCIENTISTS arrived in a Welsh village yesterday to try to solve the mystery of the exploding mountain.

Villagers of Llandrillo, Merioneth, were alarmed when a series of flashing green and blue lights in the sky and an explosion on the side of nearby Cader Bronwen, a peak in the Berwyn range.

Favourite theory at the moment is that a meteorite — a shooting star — smashed into the mountainside.

R A F photo-reconnaisance planes, which can pinpoint minute changes in ground conditions, made repeated sweeps over the mountain and the results were sent to a laboratory.

Important

Two astronomers from Keele University, Staffordshire, drove to the village at dawn to begin a search of the heather-covered mountain for tell-tale marks of a meteorite.

Senior lecturer Dr Ron Madison, assisted by Dr Nye Evans, observatory curator, said: 'We believe this would be a very important find—if we could find anything.

'It is likely to weigh about a ton. It will be about 4,000 million years old and came through Space from between Mars and Jupiter to hit the Earth.

'The crater could be anything from 5ft. to 50ft. across unless it smashed into pieces on impact.'

They recruited village boys as a line of 'beaters' to search the mountain for traces of the meteorite, and plan to resume today.

Mrs Harmsworth hands over the chain of office to Mr Coote.

'Drug peddlers at church club'

THE leaders of a 'big drugs organisation' were inside a church youth club when police launched a massive raid, it was alleged in court yesterday.

Their names were among more than 100 taken when uniformed police, CID and drug squad officers raided the Kaleidoscope Club in Kingston, Surrey.

Magistrates at Kingston were asked to take into consideration the fact that five people had died from overdoses of soft drugs in the last year and this was 'not unconnected' with the centre.

Mr Michael Stuart-Moore, prosecuting, told the magistrates 'how a police force with dogs raided the Baptist-run club on December 14.

'This was a most serious operation,' he said, 'but the defendants before the courts were only minors in the affai...'

bodies. There was a mass of people, at least 100, within a space of nine by six yards. I showed my warrant to the club leader, the Rev. Eric Blakebrough, and we started the search.'

A 22-year-old girl was given a conditional discharge for a year after admitting having cannabis. A 21-year-old man was fined £5 and bound over to £100 to be of good behaviour for having amphetamines and another man received a one-year probation order after being convicted of obstructing a policeman.

Fourteen other defendants were remanded until February 21

The top mi

MILKMAN of the Year Mr Victoria Road, New Barnet, presented with a £250 cheque

[right column partial text:]
MR wo fes ma ver Ins enc yes ing £1 chi

A Lo wif Ha t h pap sen den wit ate rec

M tha sho pro

'I war iast con she bro nes

'T tha ma suc fun

T Har app John ma New

A wor very fun.

M Har mat don a go

H alrer film Gid Redl at tl Squ Mone pren betw Vari Brita

Members of the public, intrigued by the media reports, now began to converge on Llandrillo. Some came just as tourists, never having heard of Llandrillo before. Others arrived with the intention of asking the villagers questions and doing their own private investigation into the noise and lights.

Phil Ledger visited the area on the 24th and later commented to Fortean Times, "At the village of Llandrillo I found four mountain rescue people, two of who had done a couple of searches in their Landrover, but as they were now sure it wasn't an aircraft they were rapidly losing interest." Ledger also witnessed the amount of media attention the event had generated and wryly observed: "There was an enormous crowd... of reporters, and photographers photographing reporters!" Could a large and intensely curious media presence really have failed to find evidence of a covert military operation in the area or indications of roads and land being cordoned off? [xii]

On the 25th January, the media really hit its stride with over thirty newspapers covering the Berwyn events. Though the IGS in Edinburgh had stated an earthquake was responsible, their uncertainty as to its cause led many newspapers to persist with the idea that the 'quake could have been caused by a meteor. In the minds and imaginations of professionals and members of the public it was still possible that a valuable meteorite lay somewhere on the mountains, waiting to be found by anyone adventurous enough to brave the terrain and the elements.

Friday the 25th and then the weekend of 26/27 January saw a large influx of visitors into the region, mainly to search for the meteorite the papers were still claiming might have impacted on the Berwyn Mountains. Dr Henderson from Manchester University brought a party of searchers on the 25th but they found nothing. By Saturday the 26th, the weather had turned foul but this failed to deter the intrepid searchers.

Dr Rowlands, geography tutor at Liverpool's Ethel Wormald's College, organised a party of four and they set off from Llandderfel at 10.00 a.m. in order to scour the mountainsides. Joanna McHatton, one of the students in the group, recalls, "The weather was atrocious- high winds and heavy rain, which appeared to be falling horizontally."

They saw no one all day and certainly no evidence of land being cordoned off or of a military presence of any kind. [xiii] Perhaps inevitably, the language which was used by some of the newspapers began to hint at the possibility of something much stranger than either an earthquake or a meteor. *The Daily Express* article on event the referred to it being caused by "The Thing", an RAF slang term used for UFOs in the 1949s and early 1950s until the more popular "flying saucer" gained popularity.

Opening with "The thing from outer space..." the Express's news feature gave a balanced account of what had taken place on the 23rd but added a hint of mystery by continuing, "... dropped in on Britain at just about the time that the country experienced its biggest earth tremor for two years. Result: A coincidence that produced a mystery flash and bang that startled thousands on Wednesday night." I will explore this "coincidence" in a later chapter.

The Daily Mail made the most overt reference, albeit tongue in cheek, to the involvement of extraterrestrials. Cartoonist 'mac' captured both the mysterious and topical elements of the event, depicting it as being caused by a crashed spaceship. The craft's stereotypical alien occupant, carrying a bag full of coal, was met by police and mountain rescue team who say, "That's put the cat among the pigeons – it wasn't a meteor, it's someone selling coal."

One paper in particular, the *Border Counties Advertizer,* seemed to have taken little notice of the rational and evidence interpretations of earth tremor and meteor shower. They asked,

> "Questions left unanswered are: What were the mysterious lights seen by the police on the Berwyns immediately after the rumble: what was the flaming ball shaped by the coastguards at Holyhead about an hour after the rumble; what was the object seen hovering over the Berwyns by a Gobowen family on the evening of the day after the mystery quake and why has the search been called off so quickly? One would have expected a search to go on for weeks or even months when such a large area is involved."

A search for what? The Advertizer didn't say but referred conspiratorially to a:

> "... report that an Army vehicle was seen coming down the mountain near Bala Lake with a large square box on the back of it and accompanied by outriders." [xvi]

The authorities may have been prepared to accept that an earthquake and meteor were responsible for the core phenomena on the previous evening, but author Gavin Gibbons of Shrewsbury, who had set his 1958 fictional flying saucer story on the Berwyn Mountains was not so easily convinced. He said that meteors usually gave off colours ranging from red to orange to white, and believed that was seen at 10.00 pm could be a flying saucer. [xvii]

After the weekend of 26/27 January, the media had largely lost interest in the events in Llandrillo and the Berwyn Mountains. Life in and around Llandrillo returned to normal, the events slowly fading from the villagers' minds. But the complex series of mysterious events and the ambiguity surrounding the causes provided firm foundations on which a UFO legend was soon to develop. Firstly, however, the problem of the "mysterious visitors" to the area needs to be explored. Just who were these people and what were they doing in the Llandrillo area for several days?

NOTES

i.   Interview with AR 21/2/98
ii.   Interview with AR 30/1/98

iii.   Interview with AR 31/1/98
iv.   Letter to AR, 20/12/97
v.   Colwyn Bay Police Operations Room message 9.10 a.m. 23/1/1974
vi.   MIL entry 18, p 5, 24/1/74
vii.   Colwyn Bay Police Operations Room message 10.50 a.m. 23/1/1974
viii.   MIL entry 19, p 5, 24/1/74
ix.   *Shropshire Star*, 24/1/74
x.   *Liverpool Daily Post*, 24/1/74
xi.   Letter to AR, 20/12/97
xii.   Giant Fireball, Phil Ledger, *Fortean Times* vol. 4 no. 5
xiii.   So, what was it? Joanna Mollhatton, *Denbighshire Free Press*, 26/2/98
xiv.   *Daily Express*, 25/1/74
xv.   *Daily Mail*, 28/1/74
xvi.   *Border Counties Advertizer*, 30/1/74
xvii.   *Shropshire Star*, 24/1/74

CHAPTER EIGHT

A STRANGE AND MYSTERIOUS UNIVERSE?
Earthquakes, meteors, and coincidence

There are no coincidences, but sometimes the pattern is more obvious
Neil Innes

The evening of Wednesday 23 January 1974 was a night of wonder and mystery, when signs and portents in the form of an earthquake and meteors occurred in the Berwyn Mountains. Not only that, but the two phenomena occurred more or less simultaneously at 8.38 p.m. It was the terrific explosion, the noise and the physical sensations caused by the earthquake, coupled with the almost immediate sighting of a long lasting meteor that convinced many people near the Berwyn Mountains that an aircraft had crashed. Later, when the event had mutated into the 'Berwyn Mountain UFO Legend', that same justification was used by people who believed a UFO had crashed.

The explanation by both seismologists and astronomers that the earthquake and meteor were unconnected has been repeatedly challenged by those who cannot accept that the two such significant events could be separate. But incredibly bright meteors and instances of earthquakes being accompanied by meteors are not as rare as may be thought. It is instructive, in the context of the Berwyn events, to have a brief look at some examples of extremely bright meteors and where earthquakes and meteors have been observed together. But first I am going to examine exactly how it was determined an earthquake had taken place, and to suggest some explanations for the fanciful stories which arose in its aftermath.

DID THE EARTH MOVE FOR YOU?

The earthquake was initially detected by LOWNET, the main seismographic monitoring network for the UK and recorded as being about 4ML, a reasonably powerful 'quake for the UK. Within hours of the earthquake on 23 January the Institute of Geological Sciences (later, the British Geographical Survey) Made the decision to mount a thorough investigation. A four-man team was quickly convened and sent to the Berwyn Mountains to conduct interviews with as many people as possible. The team, which consisted of Chris Browitt, Roy Lilwall, Bob McGonigle and Joe (surname unknown), arrived on 26 January, eager to gather details while the events of two days earlier were still fresh in people's minds. [i]

Each member of the team was allocated an area, and went from door to door; interviewing people about the effects that they might have felt from the earthquake. The IGS team used a standard form featuring seventeen questions, ranging from basic details such as the name and location through to questions about the physical effects on property or possessions to more abstract queries such as "Were you at all alarmed or frightened?" [ii]

If an individual answered the door when the investigator called, they would ask the questions and record the answers in their field notebooks on the spot, together with any supplementary information or, as in Pat Evans' case, drawings. If the householder was out the questionnaire was posted through the letterbox in the hope it would be completed and were returned to Dr. Willmore at the Global Seismology Unit in Edinburgh.

To gather as broad a selection of accounts as possible, the questionnaire was also published in several local and regional newspapers including the *Liverpool Daily Post* (Merseyside and Welsh editions), *North Wales Weekly News*, *Rhyl Journal and Advertiser*, *Western Mail* as well as the *Daily Mirror*, a national paper with a huge readership.

Most of the 448 questionnaires, from 112 locations, contained straightforward responses. A few, mainly from the Llandrillo area, recorded details of lights seen either in the sky or on the mountains before and after the earthquake. A handful contained comments that illuminate how perception of a natural event can create an apparently paranormal experience. As an example of this, one respondent, who was living in Old Colwyn at the time of the earthquake, wrote on her form that her door had rattled and she "... went to see if it had been forced open. There was no wind, but I had the sensation that some force had passed through my hallway." [iii]

Each interviewee or respondent was marked on a map and given a number, e.g. C74. From analysing the interview and questionnaire responses, the IGS were able to determine that the epicentre of the earthquake as being more or less under the stone circle of Moel ty Uchaf! A subsequent analysis in 1980 placed the epicentre a few kilometres further east while a 1988 study, using a broader range of seismographic sources, placed the epicentre just 7 km west of Corwen. So while the exact epicentre of the earthquake remains elusive, three separate studies were satisfied an earthquake had taken place in the area of the Berwyn Mountains. [iv]

MEN IN BLACK?

The 'Berwyn Mountain UFO crash legend' holds that in the days following the earthquake rumours spread among the villagers of Llandrillo, Llandderfel and Corwen of mysterious "officials" staying in pubs in the area, including the *Crown Hotel* in Corwen. Val Walls wrote:

> "There were people staying at the local pub who didn't bother with anybody. There were two guys staying there but they never came into the pub. They slept there. They didn't communicate with anybody;

· UNIVERSITY OF LEICESTER

DEPARTMENT OF ASTRONOMY
and HISTORY OF SCIENCE

UNIVERSITY ROAD
LEICESTER LE1 7RH
Telephone 0533 50000

Dr. C. ... Arrowitt,
Institute of Geological Sciences,
Geophysical Laboratories,
5 South Oswald Road,
Edinburgh,
EH9 2HX.

25th March 1974

Dear Dr. Arrowitt,

.... thank you for the possibilities,
and ... we're fascinating ... ...

There are no real observations of the comet. I have
compared the ... ... with the accounts we have and the impression
I have is that there must have been bright meteors at 7.25-7.3,
7.45, 7.50 and a really spectacular one at 9.50-10.0. In
addition there are at least four reports of sometimes associated
with the sounds in the showers. (Two accounts say a ball
of fire and two or three say sheet lightning of several
seconds duration).

Thanks again, keep us posted on your work,

Derek W. Sears.

Leicester Uni letter regarding meteor showers

EVENING SENTINEL 25-1-74

KEELE PROBE INTO 'FIREBALL' CONTINUES

A GROUP of astronomical scientists from Keele University returned today to the Berwyn mountain range in North Wales in a further search for what went bump in the night.

In 5½ hours' searching yesterday for what caused Wednesday evening's "explosion" or "thump," the group drew a blank. But two communications today—a phone call and a letter—gave new weight to the theory that the blast was caused by a falling meteorite.

Scientists comb 'blast' region

THE SEARCH by scientists from Keele University for the cause of the "explosion" in the North Wales mountains was today continuing unabated.

Yesterday Keele astronomer Dr. Ron Maddison spent an hour in a helicopter provided by Granada Television in an area round Llandrillo—and saw nothing to indicate that a meteorite had fallen in Wednesday evening's "explosion" or "thump."

But he pointed out that there was an area in the region —the Berwyn Mountains— that was too difficult to get to.

And he added: "A little group of four or five of our students have gone out today, and if they are unsuccessful, a bigger group will go out tomorrow. We still have not given up hope."

Referring to reports describing a "thump," Dr. Maddison said: "The geologist Dr. David Matthews is still reasonably convinced that it was an impact rather than an earth tremor. That is my feeling as well.

"We won't give up until we have scoured every bit of the region."

Dr. Maddison went on: "I am keeping an open mind. My personal subjective feeling is that it is a meteorite. The evidence is not conclusive, but tends to favour the seismological one."

Dr. Ron Maddison, Keele University astronomer and senior lecturer in physics, said that up to receiving the two communications, reports of what "certainly looked like a fireball" travelling in the direction of the Berwyn mountains, "the thing had looked very much as if it could have been an earthquake."

He added: "It looks as if Eskadalemuir Seismic Station detected this thump in the area, but I don't think they fixed its exact position or the depth."

Commenting that his party "might have been searching in the wrong area yesterday" and that they now had "added information and better bearing equipment," Dr. Maddison went on: "If there is the slightest chance of finding a meteorite, however slight, we want the thing back here."

With Dr. Maddison on today's North Wales expedition were his wife Grace; Dr. Aneurin Evans, Keele Observatory curator; and final-year student John Fletcher.

Trailing a bump in the night

SCIENTISTS moved into a Welsh village yesterday trying to solve the riddle of the thing that went bump in the night.

Two theories were advanced for the flashing lights and the apparent explosion.

Either a huge meteorite smashed into the 2,970ft Cader Berwyn in the Berwyn Range above Llandrillo, Merioneth, or the appearance of a meteorite over northern Britain coincided with an earthquake.

If a meteorite were responsible the recording would prove it to be one of the biggest ever to have struck this country.

The earthquake theory is based on the fact that Llandrillo lies over the Bala fault —a crack in the Earth's crust stretching to Cardigan Bay.

Two astronomers from Keele University, Stafford-shire, began searching the mountains area yesterday.

they definitely kept themselves to themselves. I remember seeing them but I don't remember anybody talking to them. It was a few days before these people went, a good few days." [v]

These 'strangers' have been elevated in the Berwyn Mountain UFO legend to the status of government officials gathering information about the UFO crash or - worse - 'Men In Black' sent to silence witnesses. So, who were they? If they were indeed 'Men in Black' they were so successful in their mission that no-one has come forward to report being 'silenced'. Indeed, no-one has mentioned strangers knocking at their door, or asking to speak to them. It is known from newspaper accounts, that several scientists from all over the UK visited the Berwyn Mountains in the days following the earthquake, mainly to look for evidence of the meteorite which many believed had fallen to earth. These professionals must have stayed somewhere, in local hotels and they may be responsible for some sightings of 'mysterious strangers'.

However, a much more likely source for the stories of mystery men is that they were the IGS team. They stayed in hotels in the area for a period of five days, departing on 30 January. It is unknown exactly where they stayed but Chris Browitt's notes record "Bala accommodation" with no other information, and the "*Berwyn Arms Hotel*, Glyndyfrdwy", a small village out-side Corwen. [vi] They may also have used other hotels and it is likely that the "mysterious strangers" were either the IGS investigators or other scientists investigating the meteor and earthquake. Had scientists stayed in the area at any other time than in the immediate aftermath of the earthquake and meteors it is unlikely they would have warranted a second glance. But the entire area was in a heightened state of awareness and the local inhabitants, used to their daily routine, were, because of the events of 23 January, hypersensitive to anything even slightly out of the ordinary.

COINCIDENCE? SYNCHRONICTY OR SOMETHING ELSE?

It is obvious in retrospect that the Berwyn events were triggered by an earthquake. But at the time, it was perceived as series of mystery noises and physical sensations. The earthquake, accompanied by a meteor shower, one of which was seen within seconds of the 'quake caused many people to believe there was a causal connection between the two phenomenon. This assumption might have been a natural one at the time, but it has driven the belief a landing or crashing UFO was what was seen and heard. But earthquakes and unusual aerial phenomena taking place simultaneously are not uncommon. By far the most thorough and imaginative chronicler of this kind of unusual natural phenomena was philosopher Charles Fort, the com-pulsive chronicler of anomalies. Fort many spent years of his life trawling through newspapers and recording phenomena that did not fit our accepted view of the world.

If the idea that a simultaneous earthquake and a meteor could lead people to believe a UFO had crashed then an event from October 1661 might put things in perspective. Following an earthquake and sightings of "monstrous flaming things" in the sky, a Mrs. Margaret Petmore reputedly went into labour and "brought forth three male offspring, all of whom had teeth and spoke at birth".

Did that really happen? Well, it is reported as having done so yet, as with the Berwyn Mountain UFO Legend, there is no evidence other than rumour in support of the claim. UFOs and aliens were not part of the seventeenth century's catalogue of wonders, but freakish births were. Each age, it seems, interprets the unknown in way that is culturally acceptable. [vii]

Perhaps the most dramatic case of an earthquake accompanied by a meteor comes from 1896. On 17 December of that year, at 5.30 a.m., a large meteor passed over the Hereford and Worcester area. It was bright enough to illuminate the landscape. At exactly the same time as an earthquake struck. No talking babies, or UFOs for that matter, were recorded. But at least one person is reported as dying from shock. [viii]

On 16 December 2009, an earthquake of magnitude 3.5 was registered, and a few seconds afterward a bright fireball meteor streaked across the sky in the United States. As with the Berwyn events, the media went wild. Although many people expressed astonishment about the timing of this pairing of natural phenomena it was not attributed to a UFO. The University of Nebraska's State Museum Planetarium Coordinator Jack Dunn said it was a coincidence but then reflected, "The meteor sightings happened after the earthquake, so if it had been before, then you could say well maybe it was related, but happening afterwards, probably not,". Some websites noticed this comment and suggested that perhaps it wasn't a coincidence after all. In the same way the Berwyn Mountain UFO Legend grew from minor doubts such as this, a UFO story may yet arise from the Nebraska sighting. [ix]

When nature creates a *son et lumiere* of cosmic proportions it seems that our critical faculties are, to a degree, overridden by what can only be described as awe. This awe can often act like a vacuum, sucking in theory and speculation in order to explain the improbable perceptions experienced by witnesses. It appears that each combination of an earthquake and a meteor creates a cultural Petrie dish in which belief can, but not always, flourish. This belief, it seems, can take a multiplicity of forms, such as talking babies or UFOs. Furthermore, there is no way of telling from which of these events a belief will emerge and spread, it is as random as the events themselves.

Film footage of a meteor filmed on 14 April 2010 in southwestern Wisconsin 14 April 2010 demonstrates how easy it is would have been for villagers in the Berwyn events to link the meteor and the earthquake the meteor and extrapolate it into a crashed aircraft. Witnesses to the lights after the Berwyn earthquake speak of them lasting for minutes (although equally as many said they lasted seconds). The Wisconsin meteor lasted fifteen seconds, lit up the landscape, gave a gigantic flash like sheet lightning. [x] This is highly reminiscent of the light that stunned the police and farmers as they searched the slops of the Berwyns later in the evening of 23 January.

Another meteor, from 9 October 1992, was filmed for almost thirty seconds. This one was bright green, similar to some of the meteors seen on 23 January 1974. A search of YouTube using 'meteor' as the keyword will bring up scores of filmed examples of meteors. Each one is visually astonishing in its own right when seen from the comfort of one's armchair, even in the certain knowledge that they are watching a meteor. Imagine what someone in, for instance, Llandrillo might have felt - a huge rumble passing beneath them, their houses shaking, a huge explosion. Rushing outside they look up and see a huge bright light arcing low across the sky, appearing to plummet into the mountains. No matter that the sequence of events - the light was seen after the noise and explosion - the two events become causally linked, and cemented because of the poacher's lights seen on the hillside for a while afterwards.

It is a fact that meteors are observed and earthquakes take place. It would be more unusual were the two phenomena not occasionally recorded as occurring at the same time. Set in the broader context of the history of simultaneous earthquakes and meteors, the Berwyn event seems less a one-off occurrence and more a part of a completely random sequence of events. Or, if it is part of a pattern, it is one too vast for us to determine within the conventionalities of modern science.

That these events are invested with import and meaning says a great deal about the human desire to imbue natural events with cosmic significance. Thousands of years ago, meteorites were worshipped in many parts of the world. Indeed the black stone embedded into the eastern corner of the Kaaba in Mecca, towards which devout Muslims pray, is widely believed to be a meteorite. For all our much vaunted modern science and logic, when it comes to belief and the basis on which beliefs are formed and held, how much different are humans now from how we were in prehistoric times? UFOs and the Berwyn UFO specifically are yet another symbol in a long line of symbols conjured by psyche and culture to explain the deep awe we feel when confronted with natural forces which override the flimsy logic of our rational minds.

NOTES

i.   The Enigmatic Bala Earthquake of 23 January, 1974, Roger Musson, BGS, Edinburgh
ii.   Survey of Welsh Earth Tremor, published in *Daily Mirror*, January 1974
iii.   Letter from Rhian Evans, 23/2/98
iv.   The Enigmatic Bala Earthquake of 23 January, 1974, Roger Musson, BGS, Edinburgh
v.   The Berwyn Mountain UFO Incidents, Margaret Fry, Welsh Federation of Ufologist Newsletter, no date
vi.   Notes made by Chris Browitt, BGS collection
vii.   *New Lands*, Charles Fort, JB Publishing, 1996, p. 169
viii. *New Lands*, Charles Fort, JB Publishing, 1996, p. 171
ix.   http://www.youtube.com/watch?v=txgX3CyYRO4
x.   http://www.youtube.com/watch?v=B17TmSSb5al

CHAPTER NINE

THE MAKING OF A LEGEND

"First get the facts then you can distort them all you want"
Mark Twain

The preceding chapters have outlined the events that eventually gave rise to the 'Berwyn Mountain UFO Legend', followed by a detailed examination of what really took place on the night of 23 January 1974. It would be simple to leave it at that and go straight to the conclusion. But before we do so I believe it is instructive to try to untangle just how a series of disparate natural phenomena and speculative rumour became forged into the widely held belief that a UFO piloted by aliens had crashed on the Berwyn Mountains.

As noted earlier, at the time of the Berwyn event only the *Daily Mail* referred to UFOs being involved, albeit in a satirical cartoon reflecting the political concerns of the 3 day week. If the Berwyn events had taken place in any of the past three decades, then there is no doubt that the media would have immediately have wildly speculated about UFOs. But in 1974, UFOs were past the peak of their 1950s and 60s cultural popularity and we were still some way from Spielberg's classic UFO film *Close Encounters of the Third Kind*, which heralded a new dawn for the UFO subject.

So, just how did the events of 23 January 1974 turn into 'The Welsh Roswell', as the case has been referred? To understand the matter fully it is really necessary to understand not only what *actually* took place that winter's night in 1974, but also to appreciate how the events mutated into a UFO case. In doing so, it is possible to separate the signal from the noise, the facts from the fictions and in this chapter, I examine how the Berwyn events spread from being a local-ised public disturbance and national media mystery to one of the world's most notorious crashed UFO stories.

As the story developed, it slowly moved away from the original, largely factual, media report-age and became essentially a folk tale, a story or legend traditionally passed on by word of mouth, but with the 20th century additions of the medium of books, magazines, internet and TV. As with all folktales and legends, each re-telling provided the opportunity for new strands of lore to be introduced, each addition slightly changing elements or emphasis of the story. It is from the accretion of these layers of folklore that the Berwyn Mountain UFO Legend has grown.

PUBLISH AND BE DAMNED!

Fortean Times is now an internationally known magazine dealing with all aspects of strange phenomena. In 1974, it was a duplicated fanzine with a few hundred readers. But it holds the honour of being the first printed source other than the local and national press to mention the Berwyn event. Its March 1974 issue covered the events and gave a rundown of the major news stories and theories about earthquakes and meteors. UFOs were not mentioned but various writers referred to sightings of other bright meteors in the recent past that had caused something of a disturbance to members of the public. Interestingly, the magazine also discussed the odd links and coincidences between earthquakes and sightings of meteors which. These will be examined in a later chapter. Essentially, *F.T.* gave a balanced view of what had taken place, acknowledging the facts while still allowing for an element of mystery to pervade the events.

The Ley Hunter (TLH), another small circulation magazine with its roots in the hippy generation, was another early printed source other than newspapers to refer to the puzzling events. *TLH* concerned itself with mysteries and folklore relating to prehistoric sites and the possibility that some of these sites were intentionally aligned, with a combination of other sites, landscape features or the sun, moon and stars. The March 1974, edition featured a short article on the Berwyn mystery, commenting on its resolution as an earthquake and noting the connection between the epicentre of the 'quake and the many ancient sites in the area. The article made no mention of UFOs but as an addendum, the editor noted the rumour that a wartime ammunition dump had exploded and that "the authorities were keeping quiet about it". This is the first hint at any form of government conspiracy surrounding the events. It would not be the last.

July's issue of *Fortean Times* featured a lengthy article on the Berwyn events, by William Porter. Rumblings from Arthur's Table examined the case in some depth, analysing the media reports and the coincidence of earthquake and meteors. Porter also discussed the presence of the many megalithic sites in the Llandrillo area and specifically that of Moel ty Uchaf, the cairn circle on the slopes of Cader Bronwen.

Some years after the 1974 events, artist Keith Critchlow told author Paul Devereux two scientists who were on the Berwyn Mountains in the days following the event found "very high readings on their Geiger counter when close to the circle". Of course, without further information including readings taken from a nearby control area or a follow up this anecdote is rather pointless. But because of this yarn the notion that high levels of radiation were found and were in some way connected to the alleged UFO crash has crept into some accounts of the Berwyn legend. The presence of the enigmatic Moel ty Uchaf stone circle in the same area as an alleged UFO crash has itself caused some UFO researchers to suggest a link between the event and the site, despite their being no causal link whatsoever.

The most active UK UFO organisation in the UK during 1974 was the British UFO Research Association (BUFORA). Their National Investigations Coordinator, Ken Philips, noted the Berwyn events in BUFORA Journal. Philips kept strictly to the facts, arguing that based on information provided by seismologists and meteor experts, the explosions and rumblings heard by villagers could not possibly have been caused by a meteor impact. He concluded that an earthquake was the actual cause of the disturbances. In dealing with the lights seen, Philips acknowledged the sightings of the meteors seen in the sky, but believed that they were not connected to the earthquake. He wrote:

> "In conclusion, it would now appear that two separate natural events occurred on the evening of January 23rd 1974, which were entirely unconnected but, as often happens in the press, were lumped together under the heading of a mysterious explosion in North Wales."

Of the lights seen on the mountain, Philips introduced a new theory,

> "I would tentatively put these down to that poorly understood electrical phenomenon associated with earth movement- those strange earthlights."

GREAT BALLS OF FIRE!

The Earth light theory was developed in the 1970s, when Paul Devereux began researching the history and folklore of various kinds of unusual lights seen across the world by people of many cultures. He discovered that many widely differing cultures had traditions of unusual lights; they were often known as fairies to the Irish and other Celtic peoples; to the Welsh they were presages of death known as 'corpse candles'; Buddhists built temples where they had been seen and so on. Devereux concluded that geological strain within the Earth's crust on or near seismic faults could produce intense electromagnetic fields that created glowing bodies of light that are sometimes interpreted as UFOs. 'Earthquake lights', as they are also known by seismologists have been seen in conjunction with earthquakes for hundreds of years and have been replicated under laboratory conditions. The internet has a wealth of information about Earthlights for those who wish to explore the subject further.

Whether earthlights were responsible for any of the lights seen on the Berwyn Mountains is debatable. Misperceptions of poachers' torchlights and the meteor that disintegrated over the mountains immediately after the earthquake seem adequate to explain most of the lights. For instance, the reports of a 'white flash' or 'sheet lightning' seen seconds after the earthquake may simply have been the meteor exploding; a rare phenomenon made more mysterious by its proximity to the earthquake. The red 'fires' and 'bonfires' briefly seen on the mountain were, due to the lie of the land relative to the observers' position, actually seen in the sky. Were these earthlights? Or were they the slow moving meteor prior to its disintegration, the length of time unintentionally exaggerated by astonished observers unable to explain what they saw?

This is not an attempt to debunk the possibility that earthlight phenomena were present, but to show the range of possibilities available for misinterpretation by people shocked and frightened by a powerful earthquake. The possibility of earthlights as cause for a handful of the lights remains just that, a possibility, in lieu of positive evidence.

Flying Saucer Review (FSR), a magazine which was founded in the 1950s, during the heyday of the flying saucer era, was the first UFO magazine to deal with the Berwyn events as a potential UFO case. In their 1974 *Case Histories* issue, Eileen Buckle outlined the basic story of earthquake and lights seen in the sky and on the mountain and commented that a UFO had been seen and reported to local papers on the following evening. This report apparently came from a family in Gobowen, over twenty miles away, which saw a bright disc-shaped object in the western sky in the general direction of the Berwyn Mountains. The object was stationary and observed for over ten minutes before it was obscured by clouds. No investigation was done into this sighting, but when 'UFOs' are seen in a stationary position for several minutes the explanation is often found to be a star or planet.

Buckle ended her piece with:

> "I find it hard to believe that the above sightings could all have been meteors, and equally hard to believe, assuming they were UFOs, that their appearances around about the time of the explosion could be mere coincidence, even if the explosion was due to a natural cause- which as far as I know has not been proved."

This article was an early hint that the UFO community believed it was possible UFOs were involved in the Berwyn events. Throughout the history of UFO research in the UK, there has been a quietly desperate desire for even the slightest hint that physical UFOs may exist and be visiting earth. FSR were keen proponents of the extraterrestrial hypothesis and as such often sought mystery and conspiracy where none existed.

A PEN WRITES...

After the flurry of articles about the Berwyn events in the flying saucer and earth mysteries press of 1974, excitement died down until 1975. At that time (the 1970s) the UK had dozens of UFO research groups. These were often little more than small teams of UFO enthusiasts and there was little coordination between the disparate groups. Ufologist Jenny Randles had recently set up the Northern UFO Network (NUFON) in an attempt to coordinate the northern groups, with a magazine, *Northern UFO News* (NUN) as a vehicle for case reports, news and theories.

It was against this backdrop of regional and national UFO groups that a new organisation appeared. The Aerial Phenomena Enquiry Network (APEN) started to send communications out to a variety of ufologists. The problem was no one knew who these people were. They chose to communicate solely by letter and by sending out bizarre cassette tape recordings. There was no return address or contact number and the communications featured lots of meaningless

If the industrial action were brought to an end normal working in the coal industry was restored, then normal working could be fully and quickly restored in the rest of industry.

The letter once again set out the Government's offer of a fresh investigation into miners' pay and conditions in the future.

Mr Heath said he understood the reservation of miners in wanting more pay now rather than the promise of more in the future, but he appealed to them to accept in the interest of the miners in wanting more pay and the country as a whole.

The letter went on: "I hope your executive will conclude that in the situation I have described, the acceptance of the offer and the proposals which the Government has made would bring justice not only to the aspirations of your members but also the needs and circumstances of this country."

Mr Heath said he hoped the miners would consider the "substantial and fair" offer "very carefully" before taking a decision.

Miners' leaders arriving at union headquarters for their were greeted by more 300 placard-waving South Wales pitmen chanting "Out, out."

"We wanted to show the executive we are behind a strike," said one.

JANET REEVES

The school where 23 boys died when fire broke out.

'Meteor' stays a mystery

POLICE and an RAF mountain rescue team returned empty-handed today after searching a mist-shrouded plateau for traces of a massive explosion.

One theory was that a huge meteorite had crashed into the side of Cader Bronwen mountain in North Wales, causing shock waves which shook houses over 70 miles into Lancashire and Cheshire.

Another said the tremors must have been caused by the slipping of a subterranean rock fault.

But this did not explain the tremendous bang which accompanied the tremors.

Thousands of people reported green or blue flashes and 999 calls jammed police switchboards as far apart

as Hoylake in Cheshire, the Isle of Man, Scotland, and Anglesey.

A geological observatory in Scotland recorded a tremor described as "the largest for some time."

Two boys were critically ill in today with burns.

The rest of the 300 boarders a Heart School, Berkenbes, fled in their and bare feet as flames leapt from the gutted a dormitory.

The cause of the fire is a mystery, but it is believed to have started near the second-floor dormitory just after 11 pm.

Firemen found most of the dead boys lying in the corridors and by the windows. They apparently died from smoke poisoning before the fire reached their dormitory.

Ten boys were still in bed. Others were sprawled across the room.

The school, run by Franciscan monks, is about 45 miles north-east of Brussels.

As well as 300 boarders, 200 day boys attend the school, reputed to be one of the best in Belgium for classical studies.

Sixty-three boys were asleep in the dormitory when the fire broke out, each in his own room cubicle, separated from the others by wooden partitions. The dormitory had only one door.

"When I woke up, there was smoke all around me," one survivor said. "I heard the noise of burning wood. I grabbed my pants and started running. I don't know how I made it."

PYJAMAS

Police were alerted by a woman living nearby.

"A boy in his pyjamas banged on the door shouting, 'the college burns.'

"Other boys were running out in their pyjamas and bare feet. Neighbours took them inside and several of them were driven to homes in adjoining villages and towns," the woman added.

Father Lerno, who was in the recreation lounge with other priests when the fire broke out, said: "We all ran up there as fast as we could, but the smoke was getting very thick as we reached the dormitory. I tried to get in anyhow but the smoke was overpowering and my hair started singeing from the heat.

"I think if I had gone further, I would have collapsed."

A police spokesman added "I guess the worst had already happened by the time the alert was given."

Bodies of the victims, most of them burned beyond recognition, were taken today to a chapel at the school.

Fish is saved—by a kiss

By STUART WALSH

THE "kiss of life" from schoolgirl Janet Reeves saved Snoopy the goldfish from choking to death.

Fifteen-year-old Janet, of Harbour Farm Road, Newton, Hyde, found Snoopy lying on the gravel at the bottom of her tank. The electric air pump had stopped.

Janet popped Snoopy into

a pan of fresh water, but after brief flutter she rolled over and floated to the surface.

"Since I bought her five years ago I had grown very attached to her," said Janet. "I just could not give up hope. I took her out of the water and looked into her mouth.

"Then I saw the trouble. She had sucked a stone into her mouth and it had

wedged in one of her gills.

"I put my mouth over Snoopy's and blew," said Janet. "After four tries she moved her eyes and closed her mouth in the normal breathing fashion. So I put her back and left her swimming around happily in the aquarium."

As a souvenir, Janet has had the stone taken from Snoopy's gill set in a bracelet.

'That's put the cat among the pigeons—it wasn't a meteor, it's someone selling coal.'

25-1-74

DAILY MAIL

jargon and code numbers. Most sensible ufologists at the time dismissed them as a bunch of practical jokers wanting to stir up trouble in the subculture of northern UFO enthusiasts.

Toward the end of 1974, Jenny Randles received a letter from APEN indicating there had been a UFO landing in North Wales in January 1974. No documents were provided to substantiate any of this but APEN told Jenny they were considering whether to send her their file on the incident. However, they did make some interesting claims including the suggestions that the UFO was an alien craft that had landed and not crashed in the Berwyn Mountains.

In the late spring of 1975, APEN sent Jenny their case files on what they called "The North Wales landing- 'contact'". The official looking report was typed on APEN letter headed paper and purported to be an account of APEN's investigation into the UFO event, which included an interview with a witness, "Mr. W", who saw the craft at close quarters. Cleverly, APEN did not actually mention Llandrillo, the document simply stating the locality of the event was "LLAN..." The witness was not named but was said to be living in a large farmhouse at the base of the mountain on which the landing took place.

APEN's report claimed this witness saw a "Typical Adamski Scout Ship, with some extras", with APEN commenting that the craft was similar to the "Lake District case".

This is presumably a reference to the DATE sighting and photograph of a domed flying saucer made by Stephen Derbyshire on the slopes of Coniston Old Man in the English Lake District. The witness's physical description of the aliens was also stated to be similar to those allegedly met by George Adamski, i.e. tall, blond haired humanoid figures. Whoever was behind APEN knew that any ufologist reading the report would know exactly to what they were alluding, the implication being that the "LLAN...." aliens and their craft were the same type that had been allegedly witnessed in several locations around the world since 1952.

Readers should note that the UFO and aliens in *By Spaceship to the Moon*, Gavin Gibbons' sci-fi novel of a UFO landing on the Berwyn Mountains, to which I refer in the Introduction, were also portrayed as being like those seen by Adamski and Derbyshire. Was this a coincidence? Or were some of the APEN team seasoned and knowledgeable ufologists who were spinning a joke at the UFO community's expense?

APEN allegedly were taken by the witness to the landing site, where they found and measured imprints on the ground and took soil samples. "Mr. W" claimed that he had met the aliens and it was they who gave him APENs contact details, telling him "to contact only us". APEN clearly didn't question why aliens from another planet, solar system or dimension would have handy the contact details of an unknown group of UFO investigators and, seemingly, nor did the witness. "Mr. W" alleged a period of 15 minutes 'missing time' during his encounter with the aliens and APEN suggested that he undergo a series of hypnotic regression sessions which would be able to "uncover a great deal of information which could not be obtained otherwise". The witness told APEN the aliens told him this request would be made and he should say no, but he agreed. It was also recorded that the witness was suffering "skin irritation" and headaches in the aftermath of his encounter.

Periods of so-called 'missing time', and hypnotic regression as a method for retrieving 'lost' memories in relation to UFO encounters are now a staple of almost every UFO encounter or film. But in the 1970s, they were unknown to all but a few dedicated ufologists. APEN, whoever they were, knew exactly which buttons to press to pique the interest of some parts of the UFO community.

It would be easy to discard the APEN affair as juvenile nonsense, but for one salient point. In the legend of the Berwyn Mountain UFO, it is usually accepted that the UFO crashed. However, there are researchers, such as Scott Felton, who believe that the UFO had landed, not crashed. It is likely that Felton and others who hold similar beliefs picked the idea up from the APEN story and documents. Ufologists were aware of them for many years but they were first placed in the public domain in Jenny Randles' best selling 1995 book *UFO Retrievals*.

Although in retrospect it seems obvious that APEN were a bunch of practical jokers drawn from the ranks of ufologists in northern England, some writers have still claimed that they were a secret government UFO investigation group. Even Jenny Randles has commented that they displayed a sophisticated knowledge of the UFO subject and "has not written them off totally as crackpots" and as such, APEN occupy a small but significant niche in the folklore of the Berwyn Mountain UFO legend.

For the remainder of the 1970s, the Berwyn mystery lay dormant. Then, in 1980 *Earth Lights*, by Paul Devereux, was published. This was the first book to examine the theory that some UFO phenomena was caused by geophysical stresses. In discussing the perceived link between earthlights and megalithic sites Devereux briefly mentioned the Berwyn events, and noted the proximity of the Moel ty Uchaf cairn circle and obliquely speculating about the connection between the anecdotal radiation readings, the monument and the lights. Devereux helped to perpetuate the myth that most of the Berwyn events had not been resolved by writing:

> "Quietly, the item slipped from the news as it became apparent that
> the experts would be unable to find an explanation."

In fact, at the time Devereux wrote, scientists had explanations for all aspects of the Berwyn events, and the nurse's experience had not yet become known.

CRAWLING TOWARD LLANDRILLO

The first mention of the incident in a UFO book came in 1983 with the publication of Jenny Randles' *UFO Reality*. The veteran researcher, who was - at that time - the UK's only real professional ufologist, wrote of the case in the context of other crashed UFO stories such as the world famous Rendlesham Forest incident. Randles made it clear she didn't think the event represented a crashed UFO and briefly discussed Devereux' earth light theories that were very much in vogue, if contentious, with UK ufologists in the early 1980s.

The background hum of information about the Berwyn mystery was growing, but as yet, no one had actually done an investigation into the case. Everything that was written about the case by ufologists was solely based on the original 1974 media reports.

That situation began to change in 1983 when ufologist Margaret Fry moved to North Wales. Fry claimed to have had her own UFO experiences while living in London and was a fervent believer that UFOs were indeed alien craft visiting earth. Her interest in UFOs soon became known in the area where she moved to, and she began to gather anecdotal evidence about UFO sightings, the Berwyn events among them. In 1991, one of Fry's colleagues received a letter from a Mrs Rees-Pritchard who - in 1974 - was working in a hotel in Bala. Rees-Pritchard remembered the earthquake of January 1974 and recalled that on the following morning "suited strangers were booked into the Hotel". These mysterious visitors stayed for a week and went out every day "up the mountain". As Bala is not at the foot of any mountain it would be difficult for their destination to be known with certainty and it is known that staff from the International Geological Survey were staying in the area, along with several other scientists who were searching either for evidence of a meteorite or an earthquake.

Fry interviewed Nurse Pat Evans in 1995 and it was from that interview the claim arose that Evans was stopped by police and military officials and ordered off the mountain. Although Pat Evans vehemently denied this took place and Margaret Fry later agreed she had misunderstood what Pat told her, this canard has become a central feature of the Berwyn Legend. What's more, this idea helped underpin the idea that there was some kind of secret military and police operation that night. Again, as you have seen, there is not a scrap of evidence to support that notion.

The result of Fry's failure to tape her interview with Pat Evans eventually resulted in Jenny Randles accepting Fry's anecdotes on trust and she reproduced them in several magazines articles as well as the book UFO Retrievals. Thus, the story of Pat Evans being stopped and ordered off the mountain road by police officers and soldiers entered the public domain.

The publication of Jenny Randles' *UFO Retrievals* in 1995 brought the Berwyn mystery to the attention of thousands of people. Jenny's account of the January 1974 events mixed anecdote, UFO folklore and fact into a heady brew. For instance, she quoted an anonymous local who claimed they had been told the event was a 'plane crash, *solely* in order to keep people off the mountain, and repeated the canard that areas of the Berwyn Mountains had been cordoned off for several days. Jenny also repeated the APEN material, once again speculating that there may be more to the organisation. She also introduced other anonymous witnesses who had seen unusual lights on the Berwyns, somewhat vaguely, in "winter 1974".

This creative melding of unreferenced fact and obvious fiction made for breathless reading but only served to obfuscate what was known to have actually happened on 23 January 1974. Jenny completely misrepresented Nurse Pat Evans' experience, which she had based largely on Margaret Fry's version of events and even managed to introduce completely new elements such as "for several days the road was sealed off". Jenny concluded that "the facts" suggest that there was a massive cover up and "there is increasing evidence that this may be the best example of a UFO retrieval in Britain".

This conflation of fact and fiction formed the basis of what I call 'The Berwyn Mountain UFO Legend', outlined in chapter two. Jenny is an influential ufologist and her comments regarding the Berwyn mystery were taken seriously in many quarters, which ensured the case took root in the British UFO subculture, which was desperately seeking its own version of 'The Roswell Incident'.

UFO Retrievals was published on a wave of renewed public interest in the UFO phenomenon in the mid 1990s. This was sparked by the phenomenally successful TV series the *X Files*, which first aired on satellite to the UK in January 1994 and on BBC2 in September of that same year.

THE X FACTORY

The *X Files* portrayed UFO investigation in popular terms, suggesting there were genuine, physical UFOs of extraterrestrial origin and that governments were conducting a massive cover up of this fact. The show re-vivified UFO and paranormal research. Because of this, the media was once again full of articles about UFOs and relates subjects, and as a direct result many new UFO investigation groups sprung up at the same time as existing UFO research groups found their membership soaring. Suddenly, what had previously been a tiny subculture of obsessive hobbyists became almost a national pastime.

The mid 1990s saw a slew of glossy UFO and Paranormal magazines hitting the newsstands with titles such as *Sightings*, *UFO Reality* and *Encounters* among others. These publications, which were driven more by a desire to make money on the crest of the *X Files* than out of a genuine interest in the UFO phenomenon hauled old UFO cases out for re-evaluation. Crashed saucer tales were particularly popular and it was unsurprising that the Berwyn UFO crash would be of interest to readers of these magazines. Consequently, Jenny Randles wrote a lengthy and somewhat inaccurate article about the Berwyn Mountain event for *Sightings* magazine in March 1996 spreading the legend to several thousand people, most of whom were hitherto unaware of the event.

The Yorkshire UFO Society (YUFOS) were originally a tiny and amateur UFO organisation with an interest in crashed saucers and government cover-ups. In the mid 1990s, they were staging an annual multi-day conference and publishing a newsstand UFO magazine, UFO. UFO was often concerned more with sensationalism, publicity and the need to turn a profit than to provide factual information about the UFO subject, but their magazine and conferences acted as a clearing house for all kinds of UFO title-tattle and folklore.

THE UNKNOWN SOLDIER

YUFOS' core beliefs were driven by founder member, ex Police sergeant, Tony Dodd. Along with Margaret Fry, he shared an interest in outlandish tales of aliens and UFOs that were never backed up with any checkable information, and he was seen as someone who would believe anything, if the information fitted his beliefs. In 1996, Dodd claimed that he was contacted by a retired soldier who had been involved in the retrieval of alien bodies from the Berwyn Mountains in 1974.

Although Dodd would not reveal who this informant actually was - the name James Prescott was a pseudonym - and though Dodd did not provide a scrap of verifiable evidence to support Prescott's identity, military service or claims, the story he was given was eagerly lapped up by the UK UFO subculture. The only evidence, if it can be called that, is a statement Prescott gave to Tony Dodd, which read:

> "On the 18th January, 1974 I was stationed at a barracks in the South if England. I cannot name my unit or barracks, as they are still operational. We, that is my unit, were put on standby to move north at short notice. On the night of the 19th January 1974, we had moved up toward Birmingham.

> "Then we received orders to proceed with speed towards North Wales. We were halted in Chester in readiness for a military exercise we believed was about to take place. On the 20th January, the communications to us was 'hot'. At approximately 20.13 hrs we received orders to proceed to Llangollen in North Wales and to wait at that point.

> "On arrival our unit was split into four groups and at that time we noticed a great deal of ground and aircraft activity. At approximately 11.36 hrs we, that is myself and four others, were ordered to go to Llandderfel and were under strict orders mot to stop for any civilians. When we reached our objective we were ordered to load some cargo into our vehicles. The cargo comprised of two large oblong boxes. We were at this time warned not to open the boxes, but to proceed to Porton Down facility and deliver the boxes.

> "We set off south with our cargo and during the journey we stopped to get a drink. We were immediately approached by a man in civilian clothes, who produced an I.D. card and ordered to keep moving, and not to stop until we reached our destination.

> "We eventually reached Porton Down and moved the boxes inside the facility. Once inside, the boxes were opened by staff at the facility in our presence. We were shocked to see two creatures which had been placed inside two decontamination suits.

"When the suits were fully opened it was obvious the creatures were clearly not of this world and when examined, were found to be dead. What I saw in the boxes that day made me change my whole concept of life.

"The bodies were about five to six feet tall, humanoid in shape, but so thin they looked almost skeletal with covered skin. Although I did not see a craft at the scene of the recovery, I was informed that a large craft had crashed and was recovered by other military units.

"Sometime later, we joined up with the other elements of our unit, who informed us that they had also transported bodies of 'alien beings' to Porton Down, but said their cargo was still alive. This was the only time I was ever involved in anything of this nature. This event took place many years ago and I am now retired from the Armed Forces.

"This is a true account of those events which occurred in January 1974. I am not certain of the accuracy of the times of night.

Signed: 'James Prescott'

It is very easy to criticise 'James Prescott's' account of the Berwyn events. It completely and utterly contradicts the APEN version of events - also unevidenced, save for an anonymous and unverified report - in which the UFO landed, and took off again, whereas Prescott states that the craft had crashed. For a military unit to have retrieved a "large craft" there would have to have been numerous personnel and vehicles on the mountain, including some with lifting gear. Nothing like this was seen on the night of the event and nor were any track marks of any such vehicles noticed by searchers such as Ron Maddison on the following day. In addition, for the military to have retrieved a downed UFO without being seen they would have had to have carried out the exercise at night and to have done so, restricted access to the mountain. And there are no witnesses to a military presence or of any land being cordoned off.

Prescott's tale of transporting the alien bodies to Porton Down is also somewhat risible. The discovery of a crashed UFO containing live humanoid creatures from space would be the most momentous event in the world's history. It would be highly unlikely that these alien beings would be entrusted to four soldiers and driven to Porton Down in an army lorry! Yet despite the lack of evidence, improbable story and competing and contradictory accounts, Prescott's tale entered the ufological canon as 'truth'. Those who wanted to believe an alien craft was involved in the Berwyn events took Prescott's account to be a reflection of reality and the story began to be uncritically repeated and diversified across a wide variety of UFO media. It became a cornerstone of the Berwyn UFO legend, its repetition 'proved' that a UFO really did crash and was retrieved by the military.

Interestingly, Prescott's revelations came at a time when several key UK ufologists were also being contacted by people claiming to be ex military men with a UFO story to tell. These shady characters span a good yarn, but fell short when it came to providing evidence. But in the foetid world of UFO research, where the majority of people - even those who loudly claim to profess scepticism - are waiting for any scrap of alien evidence, these tales were lapped up and used to bolster the notions of alien presence and government cover up.

Researcher Kevin McClure dubbed Prescott and his ilk 'The Unknown Soldier' and wrote perceptively of its baleful influence of UK ufology noting:

> "Sometimes the sheer incompetence of UFO research is made obvious. There is a deep longing for a British 'Roswell', a longing not entirely fulfilled by the shabby muddle that the Rendlesham story has been allowed to become. Consequently, some 'investigators' have built up the admittedly mysterious events surrounding the 'earth tremor' on Berwyn Mountain (sic) on 20.1.74 (sic) into the landing/crash of an 'Adamski-type' UFO, with a sophisticated military recovery operation involving soldiers who recovered alien bodies".

Prescott's account enabled the 'phantom helicopters' to be woven into the Berwyn legend. The fact that whoever issued orders to Prescott's unit apparently had prior information that a UFO was going to land or crash has enabled the legend makers to infer that some phantom helicopter sightings were that of military choppers out searching for the downed craft.

Jenny Randles introduced several elements into the Berwyn legend in her 1995 book *UFO Retrievals*. A perceived silence when Berwyn was mentioned at a talk that Jenny gave in the officer's mess at RAF Shawbury in 1984 led Jenny to think there might actually be a strong possibility that a military aircraft had accidentally dropped a nuclear warhead. That there is no evidence other than Jenny's speculation but in the UFO field, when something is put in print, there is a ready army of people only too willing to believe it.

Jenny later linked this theory with a story she was told by a science journalist about a possible childhood leukaemia cluster in the Bala area. She writes:

> "Of course, as the journalist said, 'I had no idea that the Llandrillo event had occurred local to Bala 20 years before.' Given my suggestion about a nuclear incident involving an RAF plane it was now not unreasonable that he would start to wonder."

Such convoluted logic is the bread and butter of UFO writers. It makes for a wonderful story but the fall-out - of you will pardon the pun - only serves to obfuscate facts and adds to UFO legends.

Other writers, who were also ufologists, added their own unintentional smears of confusion to the Berwyn legend. Nick Redfern's 1997 book, *A Covert Agenda*, which was published on the crest of that decade's UFO fascination brought a number of other misleading elements into the Berwyn legend. A UFO sighting almost twenty-four hours later in Gobowen, over twenty miles away from Llandrillo suddenly appeared to be relevant. What had initially been just a puzzling sighting of a bright light for over ten minutes - most likely a star or planet - now, in Redfern's words became "Was this yet another unidentified aerial craft, perhaps searching for the remains of the vehicle which struck the Berwyn Mountains?." Redfern also added a twist to Pat Evans' involvement in the events. As detailed in Chapter 5, Pat telephoned the police to ask what was going on and to offer her assistance. In Redfern's version, her story is changed subtly but significantly to:

> "One interviewee was a nurse who..... received a telephone call from the police at Colwyn Bay informing her of the possibility that an aircraft had crashed on Cader Bronwen."

The suggestion that the police phoned Pat, as opposed to her phoning them, is freighted at the very least with implication that the police somehow needed a nurse at the scene, when in fact it is certain Pat phoned them to offer her services. To his credit, Redfern no longer stand by this interpretation of the evidence, and accepts he was misled by the poor research of others. But *A Covert Agenda* was published to a wide audience in both the UK and US and few who read it cared that they may be basing their opinions on this shoddy research.

The Sun, a UK tabloid newspaper with hundreds of thousands of readers, often features UFO stories and in January 1999 it printed its top ten worldwide alien crash landings. The "Berwyn Mountain Incident" was number two. Neither the article nor the arbitrary ranking actually meant anything other than an index of how well known the Berwyn Mountain UFO Legend was.

By the millennium, there were numerous versions of the Berwyn Legend in circulation. And they were interchangeable. A snippet from one version could be used to support a 'fact' from another as though one un-evidenced statement was made more 'true' if linked in some way to another. Thus, stories about radiation leaks connected with the 'crash' became 'true' because of the anomalous Geiger readings taken at the stone circle days after the event. The fact that there is no actual evidence for crash, radiation leaks or high radiation readings at Moel ty Uchaf becomes immaterial and the 'Legend' lives on. As more and more different accounts of the Berwyn events were published in books, magazines and are proliferated via TV and the internet, the theories became stranger. There is no space here to list them all and the reader is advised to search the internet where they will find a plethora of stories from the farthest shores of reality, all treated as true, all believed by a small hard core of UFO nuts.

The airing of a 2008 TV documentary about the Berwyn events, Britain's Closest Encounters, stirred up a hornet's nest of claim and counter claim. Some ufologists actually stated that they believed the TV production company, Firefly, were under instruction from the government not to use the testimony of certain researchers who believed that a physical UFO crashed.

Advance publicity stirred up local interest in North Wales and generated several newspaper articles. One journalist contacted former Ministry of Defence employee Nick Pope. Pope had run the MoD's 'UFO Desk', between 1991 and 1994. Whilst in this role he began to write two books about the UFO phenomenon that made it clear that he was a believer in UFOs and aliens. Even so, Pope gave a clear and unequivocal statement about what the MoD believed about the Berwyn events. "The documents I've seen suggest the whole Berwyn Mountain UFO crash was a combination of meteors/fireballs, a small earthquake, a search and rescue operation launched because of calls suggesting an aircraft had crashed, rumour, hysteria and the over-active imagination of certain UFO enthusiasts."

The 'documents' Pope that referred to were the much vaunted Ministry of Defence file on the Berwyn events. Those who believed a physical UFO had crashed set great store by what the MOD knew about the case but had been thwarted because the MOD had failed to release any information and worse still claimed there was no file on the Berwyn events. And they were correct. In January, 2005 when the MOD file pertaining to January 1974 was released, it was found to contain very little of interest, and certainly no revelations about crashed UFOs or alien cadavers; just a few reports of the meteors seen across the country on 23 January and some related internal correspondence. A smoking gun it was not! The conspiratorially minded immediately claimed that the 'real' Berwyn UFO file was still secret, and so the case was once again in a hall of mirrors where nothing less than the UK government's admission that a UFO piloted by aliens had crashed would satisfy the believers.

Everything that has been written or broadcast about the events in the Berwyn Mountains has had an impact on the Berwyn Mountain legend. Even the publication of this book has become part of the legend and, no doubt, my evidence-based scepticism will be subsumed into further rumours that I am a puppet of state, paid to write disinformation so the greatest story never told can remain under wraps. If that is the case then perhaps the government could take note and send me the cheque now, please!

NOTES

i.   *Fortean Times*, March 1974
ii.   *The Ley Hunter*, no. 58, March 1974
iii.   *Fortean Times*, March 1974
iv.   *Earthlights*, Paul Devereux , BCA 1982
v.   *Bufora Journal*, vol 4 no 2, 1974
vi.   http://www.pauldevereux.co.uk/
vii.   *FSR Case Histories*, no. 18, 1974
viii.   *UFO Retrievals*, Jenny Randles, Cassell 1995
ix.   Jenny Randles, interview with Nick Redfern 28 March, 1987
x.   *Earthlights*, Paul Devereux , BCA 1982

xi.   *UFO Reality*, Jenny Randles, Robert Hale, 1983
xii   The Berwyn Mountain UFO Incidents, Margaret Fry, *Welsh Federation Newsletter*
xiii.   *UFO Retrievals*, Jenny Randles, Cassell 1995
xiv.   *UFO Retrievals*, Jenny Randles, Cassell 1995
xv.   Special Report: Wales, *UFO Magazine*, Sept/Oct 1996
xvi.   Unnamed Soldiers, *Abduction Watch* nos 4/5 Nov & Dec, 1997
xvii.   Jenny Randles, Mountain Questions, November 1998
xviii. *A Covert Agenda*, Nick Redfern, Simon & Shuster, 1997
xix.   *The Sun*, 12 January, 2009
xx.   Dear UFO Enthusiast, Letter circulated to ufologists by Scott Felton, November 2009
xxi.   Britain's Closest Encounters, Firefly TV, 1998

CHAPTER TEN

THE MYSTERY OF HISTORY

"The most beautiful thing we can experience is the mysterious. It is the source of all true art and all science. He to whom this emotion is a stranger, who can no longer pause to wonder and stand rapt in awe, is as good as dead: his eyes are closed."

Albert Einstein

I t's been a long journey. From a collection of disparate, but seemingly connected, events on the night of 23 January, 1974 to a story of crashed flying saucers, retrieved aliens and a government conspiracy to conceal this from the general public. Phew!

But what really happened?

The simple answer is no one really knows. No one, the witnesses to the events, the media nor the UFO investigators who have contributed to the making of the 'Berwyn Mountain UFO legend', knows the totality of what really took place on that dark and rainy January night in 1974.

There is a mass of information about the Berwyn events, some of it factual, and some of it confusing, much of it contradictory. As I noted in the introduction, the information is like a Rubik's cube or a kaleidoscope, in that a subtle change to one element dramatically alters the overall picture. Thus, it has been my intention that the preceding chapters have given all the information in order for you, the reader, to draw your own conclusions about the Berwyn events. Who knows, you might even be right!

But it's my book, and my conclusion, and so as such, I would like to offer you my personal interpretation of what really happened. I call it, after that well-known series of books....

BERWYN FOR DUMMIES

At 8.38 pm there was an earthquake of 3.5 ML, which was centred on the Berwyn Mountains. The combination of both the characteristics of earthquakes and people's unfamiliarity with the phenomena led many to believe 'something', most probably an aircraft, had crashed on the Berwyn Mountains. As people rushed outside, in a heightened state of anxiety and in some cases outright fear, to check property and speak with neighbours they saw lights in the sky and on the mountainside. The largest of these lights was a meteor that had travelled over England and Wales before apparently disintegrating over the Berwyn Mountains. This meteor was seen by villagers in Llandrillo and Llandderfel area and was described in a variety of ways and as lasting anything from a few seconds to a few minutes. Most of the witnesses who saw this meteor automatically associated it with the earthquake, believing what they now saw was a direct consequence of what they had felt and heard only moments earlier.

There is a very small possibility some of the lights - perhaps the 'flashes', - were the luminous phenomena called earthlights, created by the geophysical strains that caused the earthquake. But it is only a very small possibility, and based on the witness statements and the opinions of seismologists, I feel it is highly unlikely. Yet it cannot be completely ruled out. The vertical beams of white light that were intermittently observed for up to twenty minutes after the earthquakes belonged to the poachers.

The police, overwhelmed by hundreds of telephone calls, initially believed an air disaster had taken place. Finding no evidence of a missing 'plane to support this, they still went to the area to try to resolve the disturbance. At least two police officers, guided by a local farmer's son, searched the lower slopes of Cader Bronwen but found nothing. In Llandderfel, Nurse Pat Evans, believing an aircraft crash had taken place, drove along the B4391 to the mountains and saw a huge light that pulsated and changed colour. The light was apparently attended by vehicles and torch lights.

At approximately 9.58 p.m., another large meteor passed overhead and disintegrated. This was seen across north Wales and of England as well as by the police officers who were searching the mountains. On the following day, the 24th, the mountains were searched again by police officers, a mountain rescue team, soldiers from a Territorial Army unit, several people from a university and interested locals. The area was also searched from the air by RAF aircraft and helicopters from national and regional TV companies. The IGS in Edinburgh confirmed an earthquake had taken place and sent a team of field investigators to the area to carry out door-to-door interviews for the purpose of gathering information to determine a more exact location of the earthquake. Because these people were formal and taking detailed notes, there was an element of suspicion about them. Consequently, their presence has been mythologised into 'Men in Black'. There was a huge amount of media excitement around the events, which soon resulted in it being featured in all the national newspapers and on national and regional TV and radio.

The following week saw the Berwyn Mountains visited and searched by literally hundreds of journalists, scientists and members of the public. Nothing whatsoever was found to indicate that anything had crashed on the Berwyn Mountains and at that time, in 1974, there was no suggestion that the events were thought to have been caused by a UFO.

As the years passed, due to the coincidence of meteor and earthquake, along with sightings of other lights, the story began to make its way into the magazines and books that catalogued mysteries. Because there was a mystery, and because the 80s and 90s saw a huge upsurge of interest and belief in UFOs, the Berwyn events slowly, but surely, mutated into the 'Berwyn Mountain UFO Legend'. Reduced to its basic elements, this Legend claimed that an alien craft had crashed or landed and the military had retrieved it and the aliens it contained, covering up the story from the public. As the story was re-told and re-written, and as the people from the Berwyn Mountain region were interviewed and re-interviewed, the legend grew and sub-divided, soon taking on a life of its own independent of the known facts.

THE HISTORY OF MYSTERY

There exists a residue of loose ends and unresolved elements in the Berwyn event. These are not necessarily mysterious in and of themselves and further research may yet determine their cause or, more likely, lure researchers down false trails. When combined these anomalies sustain the legend and add to the continuing air of mystery surrounding 23 January 1974. However, these peripheral oddities should not detract from the genuine enigma at the heart of the Berwyn events.

As I have previously noted, at one time I believed I had resolved the entire Berwyn mystery. I was convinced, based on documentary evidence, that the unusual light seen by Pat Evans was somehow connected to the police officers meeting the poachers during their search of the mountainside. I believed the light was a poacher's lamp, refracting light in the drizzle and perceived by Pat as large because of the lack of visual reference points and her expectation she was going to the site of an air disaster. Subsequently, further documentary evidence appeared which made that scenario impossible.

So, while all other elements of the Berwyn Mountain UFO Legend may be explained by the evidence presented in this book, I simply have no idea what Pat saw or, by extension, to whom the adjacent torch and vehicle lights belonged. If those lights belonged to the police officers and farmer's son then they must have seen the light that Pat witnessed, ...but they did not. No matter how I interpret the evidence, the nature of Pat's experience remains a mystery. But there are caveats to the mystery. It should be remembered that Pat only saw a two dimensional light, that was stationary on the ground, and not a UFO or indeed a solid physical object of any kind. It was just a light, albeit a huge one. And nor is there any direct connection between Pat's sighting and other elements of the Berwyn events, such as the earthquake and lights seen in the sky. There are also, as I have described, many inconsistencies regarding the location of what Pat saw.

The above factors notwithstanding, it does not mean Pat's sighting will remain unexplained. The torch and vehicles lights indicate that several people were close to the light and thus someone, somewhere, knows what it is. Perhaps the publication of this book will eventually bring forward new evidence that will tie up this significant loose end.

That's what I believe happened. What you, the reader, believe about the Berwyn events will depend on a number of factors including, but not limited to, the following:

• Whether you accept everything reported by the witnesses is objective truth, and that

people are not subject to innocent misperception.
- Whether you accept the contemporary records generated by the police, IGS, The Mountain Rescue Team etc., are accurate and reflect the events, as they were perceived and reported.
- What you believe constitutes admissible evidence, as opposed to anecdote, rumour and speculation.
- What beliefs about UFOs and aliens you hold.
- Whether you believe in the reality of a government conspiracy large enough to sustain the cover up of significant information about the Berwyn events.
- Whether you believe the natural world can sometimes conspire to create *son et lumiere* events that trigger our sense of awe and mystery but can also lead us unwittingly down into the labyrinth of belief.

Of course, I could be entirely wrong in my interpretation of the core Berwyn events and in my critique of the 'Berwyn Mountain UFO Legend'. Perhaps an alien craft did crash and, along with bodies and live aliens was indeed retrieved by the military and secretly transported to a government facility, all of which has been covered up by the political administration. If this is the case then hopefully, at least, this book will serve as a research tool enabling someone else to unearth - and prove - this alternate truth.

The world of UFO research and investigation is strange. Besides creating and sustaining the 'Berwyn Mountain UFO Legend', the UFO subculture's understanding of the events that spawned the legend is often based more in belief than in verifiable fact. Those who believe the Legend represents a physical reality and objective truth cannot countenance contrary evidence. Thus, my reasons for devoting several years to researching and writing about the Berwyn events - and not believing that it involves UFOs and aliens - has been called into question on numerous occasions.

Because of my refusal to believe that an alien craft crashed on the Berwyn Mountains, I have been called a 'debunker'. Meaning that because I do not believe aliens or UFOs exist (as if my belief would affect reality!) I have sought to rubbish the claims of those who do and have used evidence selectively to support my own beliefs. I have also been openly accused of actively working for the British government as a disinformation agent; part of the cover up to ensure that the real truth about the Berwyn incident is kept hidden. This idea manifested itself most recently in October 2009. On the Richplanet.net website, run by Richard D. Hall I, and others involved in the investigation of anomalous phenomena, were publically accused of being MI5 agents! An extract from Hall's comments reads:

> "Andy Roberts' ambition in life has been to try and explain away all UFO cases as anything but extra terrestrial in nature. Why would somebody, without the sponsorship or backing of a funding organisation do nothing except try and criticise and pour cold water on other researchers work?.... In the past there has been disinformation put out about the Berwyn case, probably by government (MI5). Because

of these incidences, we know that the authorities are paranoid about
what happened at Berwyn in 1974. If one couples this fact, with the
fact that Roberts has spent more effort trying to debunk this case
than any other. You are left with the realisation that he must be being supported by the same people that have been preventing BBC and
others from talking about the case. We believe Roberts is being
steered by the MI5 disinformation program."

Once again, the reader will have to make up their mind as to the veracity of Hall's allegations.
You may want to laugh heartily at Hall's remarks – I certainly did. Sadly, he and others like
him are so distanced from everyday reality that they really believe this sort of unsubstantiated
nonsense, which is then fed back into the UFO community, further obfuscating an already
complex subject.

HAVE YOU EVER BEEN EXPERIENCED?

Humankind needs mystery. Our religions and sciences are based on the encoding, explaining
and resolving of the central mystery of existence. And, if the sheer amount of religions, cults,
books, magazines, films and other media dealing with mysteries of all kinds is anything to go
by, humans not only need mystery but also crave it. And it is from this desire for mystery that
the 'Berwyn Mountain UFO Legend' was created from the events of 23 January 1974. Now
the Legend exists it can never be destroyed. Were all differing factions to agree on the Berwyn
events being caused by, say, misperception, the Legend would continue and would be repeated
endlessly in books and magazines with new elements of UFO-lore constantly being added to
it. Far from this being a negative thing , the persistence of the Berwyn Mountain UFO Legend
exemplifies the talent that we have to create marvellous stories, in this case stories hinting at
contact with other intelligences, other worlds, from the warp and weft of nature and the human
psyche. The 'Berwyn Mountain UFO Legend' does not end with this book and indeed this
book is now very much part of it. Those who believe aliens and UFOs will continue to do so.
As will those who believe that the Berwyn Mountains event were a complex series of natural
phenomena augmented by misperception and amplified by the media. New theories about the
events will be formed and discarded; new researchers will come and go. Life on the Berwyn
Mountains and in Llandrillo and Llandderfel will continue. Villagers and farmers will barely
notice the steady stream of visitors who come to walk the streets and mountainsides, each one
driven by their beliefs, hopes and certainties about what happened there on a winter's night
long ago.

Pat Evans and her experience are fated to remain a central part of both the Berwyn events and
the Berwyn Legend. Though she may now regret her altruistic offer of help to the police, or in
speaking to UFO researchers about what she saw, Pat has joined that select group of people
who have undergone a genuinely unexplained anomalous experience. As such, the final words
must be hers.

"But I kept thinking... we'd be told, and the mystery deepens because you're not told."

Comment or criticism of this book is most welcome and can be directed to the author, who will respond to all communications, at andy@cfz.org.uk. If you have any information about any aspect of the Berwyn Mountain UFO events Andy would love to hear from you at the above email address.

THE WORLD'S WEIRDEST PUBLISHING COMPANY

HOW TO START A PUBLISHING EMPIRE

Unlike most mainstream publishers, we have a non-commercial remit, and our mission statement claims that "we publish books because they deserve to be published, not because we think that we can make money out of them". Our motto is the Latin Tag "Pro bona causa facimus" (we do it for good reason), a slogan taken from a children's book `The Case of the Silver Egg` by the late Desmond Skirrow.

WIKIPEDIA: "The first book published was in 1988. `Take this Brother may it Serve you Well` was a guide to Beatles bootlegs by Jonathan Downes. It sold quite well, but was hampered by very poor production values, being photocopied, and held together by a plastic clip binder. In 1988 A5 clip binders were hard to get hold of, so the publishers took A4 binders and cut them in half with a hacksaw. It now reaches surprisingly high prices second hand.

The production quality improved slightly over the years, and after 1999 all the books produced were ringbound with laminated colour covers. In 2004, however, they signed an agreement with LightningSource, and all books are now produced perfect bound, with full colour covers."

Until 2010 all our books, the majority of which are/were on the subject of mystery animals and allied disciplines, were published by `CFZ Press`, the publishing arm of the Centre for Fortean Zoology (CFZ), and we urged our readers and followers to draw a discreet veil over the books that we published that were completely off topic to the CFZ.

However, in 2010 we decided that enough was enough and launched a second imprint, `Fortean Words` which aims to cover a wide range of non animal-related esoteric subjects. Other imprints will be launched as and when we feel like it, however the basic ethos of the company remains the same: Our job is to publish books and magazines that we feel are worth publishing, whether or not they are going to sell. Money is, after all - as my dear old Mama once told me - a rather vulgar subject, and she would be rolling in her grave if she thought that her eldest son was somehow in `trade`.

Luckily, so far our tastes have turned out not to be that rarified after all, and we have sold far more books than anyone ever thought that we would, so there is a moral in there somewhere...

Jon Downes,
Woolsery, North Devon
July 2010

CFZ PRESS

Other Books in Print

Tetrapod Zoology Book One by Dr Darren Naish
The Mystery Animals of Ireland by Gary Cunningham and Ronan Coghlan
Monsters of Texas by Gerhard, Ken
The Great Yokai Encyclopaedia by Freeman, Richard
NEW HORIZONS: Animals & Men *issues 16-20 Collected Editions Vol. 4* by Downes, Jonathan
A Daintree Diary -
Tales from Travels to the Daintree Rainforest in tropical north Queensland, Australia by Portman, Carl
Strangely Strange but Oddly Normal by Roberts, Andy
Centre for Fortean Zoology Yearbook 2010 by Downes, Jonathan
Predator Deathmatch by Molloy, Nick
Star Steeds and other Dreams by Shuker, Karl
CHINA: A Yellow Peril? by Muirhead, Richard
Mystery Animals of the British Isles: The Western Isles by Vaudrey, Glen
Giant Snakes - Unravelling the coils of mystery by Newton, Michael
Mystery Animals of the British Isles: Kent by Arnold, Neil
Centre for Fortean Zoology Yearbook 2009 by Downes, Jonathan
CFZ EXPEDITION REPORT: Russia 2008 by Richard Freeman *et al*, Shuker, Karl (fwd)
Dinosaurs and other Prehistoric Animals on Stamps - A Worldwide catalogue by Shuker, Karl P. N
Dr Shuker's Casebook by Shuker, Karl P.N
The Island of Paradise - chupacabra UFO crash retrievals,
and accelerated evolution on the island of Puerto Rico by Downes, Jonathan
The Mystery Animals of the British Isles: Northumberland and Tyneside by Hallowell, Michael J
Centre for Fortean Zoology Yearbook 1997 by Downes, Jonathan (Ed)
Centre for Fortean Zoology Yearbook 2002 by Downes, Jonathan (Ed)
Centre for Fortean Zoology Yearbook 2000/1 by Downes, Jonathan (Ed)
Centre for Fortean Zoology Yearbook 1998 by Downes, Jonathan (Ed)
Centre for Fortean Zoology Yearbook 2003 by Downes, Jonathan (Ed)
In the wake of Bernard Heuvelmans by Woodley, Michael A
CFZ EXPEDITION REPORT: Guyana 2007 by Richard Freeman *et al*, Shuker, Karl (fwd)

Centre for Fortean Zoology Yearbook 1999 by Downes, Jonathan (Ed)
Big Cats in Britain Yearbook 2008 by Fraser, Mark (Ed)
Centre for Fortean Zoology Yearbook 1996 by Downes, Jonathan (Ed)
THE CALL OF THE WILD - Animals & Men issues 11-15
Collected Editions Vol. 3 by Downes, Jonathan (ed)
Ethna's Journal by Downes, C N
Centre for Fortean Zoology Yearbook 2008 by Downes, J (Ed)
DARK DORSET -Calendar Custome by Newland, Robert J
Extraordinary Animals Revisited by Shuker, Karl
MAN-MONKEY - In Search of the British Bigfoot by Redfern, Nick
Dark Dorset Tales of Mystery, Wonder and Terror by Newland, Robert J and Mark North
Big Cats Loose in Britain by Matthews, Marcus
MONSTER! - The A-Z of Zooform Phenomena by Arnold, Neil
The Centre for Fortean Zoology 2004 Yearbook by Downes, Jonathan (Ed)
The Centre for Fortean Zoology 2007 Yearbook by Downes, Jonathan (Ed)
CAT FLAPS! Northern Mystery Cats by Roberts, Andy
Big Cats in Britain Yearbook 2007 by Fraser, Mark (Ed)
BIG BIRD! - Modern sightings of Flying Monsters by Gerhard, Ken
THE NUMBER OF THE BEAST - Animals & Men issues 6-10
Collected Editions Vol. 1 by Downes, Jonathan (Ed)
IN THE BEGINNING - Animals & Men issues 1-5 Collected Editions Vol. 1 by Downes, Jonathan
STRENGTH THROUGH KOI - They saved Hitler's Koi and other stories by Downes, Jonathan
The Smaller Mystery Carnivores of the Westcountry by Downes, Jonathan
CFZ EXPEDITION REPORT: Gambia 2006 by Richard Freeman *et al*, Shuker, Karl (fwd)
The Owlman and Others by Jonathan Downes
The Blackdown Mystery by Downes, Jonathan
Big Cats in Britain Yearbook 2006 by Fraser, Mark (Ed)
Fragrant Harbours - Distant Rivers by Downes, John T
Only Fools and Goatsuckers by Downes, Jonathan
Monster of the Mere by Jonathan Downes
Dragons:More than a Myth by Freeman, Richard Alan
Granfer's Bible Stories by Downes, John Tweddell
Monster Hunter by Downes, Jonathan

Fortean Words

The Centre for Fortean Zoology has for several years led the field in Fortean publishing. CFZ Press is the only publishing company specialising in books on monsters and mystery animals. CFZ Press has published more books on this subject than any other company in history and has attracted such well known authors as Andy Roberts, Nick Redfern, Michael Newton, Dr Karl Shuker, Neil Arnold, Dr Darren Naish, Jon Downes, Ken Gerhard and Richard Freeman.

Now CFZ Press is launching a new imprint. Fortean Words is a new line of books dealing with Fortean subjects other than cryptozoology, which is - after all - the subject the CFZ are best known for. Fortean Words is being launched with a spectacular multi-volume series called *Haunted Skies* which covers British UFO sightings between 1940 and 2010. Former policeman John Hanson and his long-suffering partner Dawn Holloway have compiled a peerless library of sighting reports, many that have been made public before.

Other forthcoming books include a look at the Berwyn Mountains UFO case by renowned Fortean Andy Roberts and a series of books by transatlantic research Nick Redfern.

CFZ Press is dedicated to maintaining the fine quality of their works with Fortean Words. New authors tackling new subjects will always be encouraged, and we hope that our books will continue to be as ground breaking and popular as ever.

OTHER BOOKS BY ANDY ROBERTS

Catflaps: Anomalous Big Cats in the North, Brigantia Books ,1986/CFZ 2001

Phantoms of the Sky (with David Clarke), Robert Hale, 1990

Earthlights Revelation (contributing author), Paul Devereux, Blandford, 1991

Ghosts & Legends of Yorkshire, Jarrold, 1992

Twilight of the Celtic Gods (with David Clarke) Blandford, 1996/97

The UFOs That Never Were (with Jenny Randles & David Clarke - Feb. 2000)

Out of the Shadows (with David Clarke), Piatkus, 2002

Strange Secrets (with Nick Redfern), Paraview, 2005

The Flying Saucerers (with David Clarke), Heart of Albion, 2007

Albion Dreaming: A Social History of LSD in the UK – Marshall Cavendish, 2008

Strangely Strange, but Oddly Normal – CFZ 2010

Lightning Source UK Ltd.
Milton Keynes UK
176429UK00001B/64/P